42nd Regiment

Gallipoli 1915

42ⁿᵈ Regiment Gallipoli 1915
by Ahmet Diriker

ISBN: 978-1-7753253-0-7

Publisher: Lindenbrooks Publishing
6 Belsize Drive Unit 402 Toronto
M4S 1L4 Ontario Canada
contact@lindenbrooks.com

First Edition: May 2018

Translation from Turkish: Ebru Diriker

Cover Design: Ahmet Diriker

Photograph on cover page: Officers of the 42nd Regiment at the Gallipoli Front (from the author's family album).

Copyright © 2018 by Ahmet Diriker.
All rights reserved. No part of this publication may be reproduced or transmitted in any form or by any means, electronic, mechanical, including photocopying, recording or any information storage and retrieval system, without the prior written permission of the author.

42nd Regiment
Gallipoli 1915

Ahmet Diriker

In memory of Meriç...

Contents

Preface 11

Part 1
Before August 1915

The First World War 15

The Situation in the Ottoman Empire 16

The Gallipoli Front 17

Kerevizdere Battles 19

The First Battle of Kerevizdere 20

The Second Battle of Kerevizdere 21

The Suvla Campaign 23

Intelligence on Turkish forces 24

The French role in General Hamilton's plans 24

The position of the forces in Seddulbahir on 1 August 1915 24

The Situation in the Kerevizdere valley 25

Part 2

The 42nd Regiment in the Front-Line Trenches

The Regiment arrives in Gallipoli 27

The 42nd Regiment goes to the front line 29

The position of the French forces 34

The French operation plans 35

Marking of the trenches 37

The clashes intensify 37

The British attack Seddulbahir; the French wait 38

The French attack in Kerevizdere 42

Opposite the Turkish trenches… 59

The day after the French attack 63

Change of commanders on the French side 69

The bombardment intensifies 70

Solidarity between two regiments 73

Part 3

Trench Warfare

War in deadlock 75

Raid on the Blockhouse 77

Soldiers who fall asleep out of sheer exhaustion while firing 84

Hasan Tahsin Bey 86

Osman Bey's battalion retreats 87

The Kerevizdere trenches 87

An offensive attempt against the French blockhouse... 91

The French attack back 91

Bilateral attacks continue 93

A new attack on the blockhouse 94

Handover of the battalions of the 42nd Regiment 97

Attacks on the French trenches 97

A Turkish blockhouse against the French blockhouse 98

Letter from the Turkish commander to occupying soldiers 102

Reconnaissance patrol reproaches 103

The trench that could not be dug 103

Curious enemy soldiers 104

From a cowardly soldier to the bravest 106

Intensive bombardment 108

The 42nd Regiment hands over the first line 109

Lt. Col. Fuad Bey is shot 110

14 September and its aftermath 112

The French pull forces from the Gallipoli Front 115

42nd Regiment takes over the first line again 116

Kâzım Bey leaves 122

Mine wars intensify 123

Part 4

The Road to Victory

42nd Regiment Hands Over its Trenches 125

Freezing cold weather 126

Turkish Victory 128

Nuri Bey Fountain 128

The 42nd Regiment leaves Gallipoli 129

The 42nd Regiment after the Dardanelles Campaign 131

Epilogue… 133

Annex

Documents 135

Biographies 151

References 155

Bibliography 165

Index 168

Preface

The First World War, which led to the loss of millions of lives at the beginning of the 20th century, has become entrenched in our collective memory as one of the biggest tragedies of human history. Its results have shaped the world that we live in today.

The Battle of Gallipoli was one of the most important campaigns of the First World War. Gallipoli witnessed the largest amphibious operation in world history up to that moment. A national army, defending its territory on a relatively small piece of land, had to simultaneously withstand both the naval and the land forces of the invading powers.

The outcome of the Gallipoli Campaign had major consequences on world events, such as the fall of Czarist Russia. The Turks, on the other hand, who had suffered significant losses in the Balkan Wars, emerged from Gallipoli with a renewed sense of self-confidence. Mustafa Kemal (Atatürk) emerged as a military genius, and the respect and reputation he earned for himself in the Dardanelles allowed him to lead the masses in Anatolia – although he would be stripped of his titles and sentenced to death for starting the War of Independence, which he would ultimately go on to win.

42 high-ranking commanders of Gallipoli would also play active roles in the War of Independence. In many ways, Gallipoli prepared the high-ranking cadres of officers for their roles in the War of Independence.[1]

42nd Regiment

The 42nd Regiment, which is the focus of this book, was an important military unit that served not only in Gallipoli, but also in the defence of Medina and in the Turkish War of Independence. During the Gallipoli Campaign, it was stationed at Kerevizdere in the Seddulbahir area.

Although Kerevizdere (also referred to as 'the French Sector' in international literature) was a major battlefield which witnessed tough battles with high casualties – not dissimilar from Anafartalar, Kirte and Zığındere – it has found significantly little place in both the national and international literature on the First World War. One possible reason behind this could be Kerevizdere's non-canonical status in French historiography. Gallipoli was only one of many fronts where the French fought in the war, and one that ended with a defeat. Most French writings from the era have focused on the Western front that is closer to home than the more distant Gallipoli. Especially after the French involvement in the Second World War, interest in the Gallipoli Campaign declined significantly.[2]

In contrast to France, the victory at Gallipoli was always considered a major landmark in Turkish history. Numerous books have been written on the topic. And yet, there is still a need for research based on archives and original documents, rather than a repetitive glorifying narrative.

To this end, this book has made a concerted effort to explore the role of the 42nd Regiment in the Gallipoli Campaign based on original documents. Extensive research was conducted in the Turkish Military Archives (Military History and Strategic Studies Division of the General Staff - Askeri Tarih ve Stratejik Etüd Daire Başkanlığı, ATASE) and the French Military Archives (Service Historique de la Défense).

The main narrative of the book relies on the war diaries of the 42nd Regiment. This is complemented by references from the war diaries of other Turkish troops, war diaries and correspondence of the French forces located across from the Turkish forces at Kerevizdere, as well as personal memoirs.

It is interesting to note that while Turkish war diaries are very detailed in their account of daily events, the French war diaries are generally quite brief. My observation regarding the level of detail in these documents aligns with the argument in Gallipoli literature that the Ottoman forces had better 'situational awareness', which possibly enhanced their 'combat effectiveness' and played a critical role in the Turkish victory at Gallipoli.[3]

For the general reader who might not be very familiar with the subject matter, I have tried to provide some historical context in Part 1 by briefly summarizing the sequence of events from the start of the First World War up to the arrival of the 42nd Regiment in Gallipoli. In other sections, the narrative has been almost exclusively based on original documents. There are many direct quotations from Turkish war diaries. These quotations are referenced at the end of each sentence. If the whole paragraph relies on the same reference, the reference is placed at the end of the paragraph.

While the Turkish edition of this book keenly preserved the original writing style of the original documents, their translation into English has inevitably introduced some differences, especially with regards to register and polite grammatical forms. The translation has retained the original forms of address used in the Ottoman military hierarchy, such as 'Bey' and 'Efendi' which were added to the ranks and names of officers. Any additions or explanations to the original texts made by the author have been placed inside square brackets.

I am hoping that this work will be a small contribution to commemorating Mustafa Kemal Atatürk and the thousands of fallen soldiers in

42nd Regiment

Gallipoli. I would like to pay special tribute to the soldiers of the 42nd Regiment and its commander Ahmet Nuri Diriker, my grandfather.

Many people have contributed directly or indirectly to this book. I would like to thank Melike Bayrak for encouraging me to work on the Gallipoli Campaign, my father Ali Fuat Diriker for enriching my research with his ideas, Mesut Güvenbaş for always offering his help, Ahmet Arısan for his support, Karolina Dejnicka for proofreading the translation, and the staff at ATASE for facilitating my research in the military archives.

My special thanks go to my wife, Dr. Ebru Diriker, for her unwavering support, and for gracefully surmounting the challenge of translating this book. My sons, Kaan and Hakan, passing this book on to you was my real source of inspiration and motivation.

I dedicate this book to the memory of my niece Meriç Soylu, whom I lost far too young.

Ahmet Diriker
May 2018

Part 1

Before August 1915

The First World War

In the last quarter of the 19th century, Germany and Italy had succeeded in securing political unity, but had largely failed at securing a share in the European colonization process. When they finally started to push in this direction, it shook the sensitive balance of power hitherto established between the major powers of Great Britain, France, Austria-Hungary and Russia. Germany managed to attain rapid industrialization and economic growth and became a major threat to British and French interests. Relations between Russia and Austria-Hungary, on the other hand, were already tense because of their rivalry for more power in the Balkans.

At the beginning of the 20th century, new alliances emerged with Britain, France and Russia on one side, and Germany, Austria-Hungary and Italy on the other. By 1914, the political climate had turned very hostile. Europe was like a ticking bomb waiting to explode.

The final spark that ignited war was the assassination of Franz Ferdinand, the heir to the Austrian throne, and of his wife by a Serbian nationalist on 28 June 1914 in Sarajevo. Austria declared war on Serbia when the latter rejected an ultimatum. Artillery fire across the borders of these two countries was only the beginning of a long and bloody war that would last four years and cost around 20 million lives.

The Situation in the Ottoman Empire

After its catastrophic defeat in the Balkan Wars in 1913, the Ottoman Empire had lost not only most of its territories in Europe, but also a significant part of its elite forces. The Empire was suffering political, military and economic setbacks. The major European powers still had their eyes on the remaining territories of the crumbling Empire. The Russians wanted the Bosphorus and Dardanelles Straits, which would grant them access to open seas. The Germans, on the other hand, were following Otto von Bismarck's policy of 'eastward expansion,' and sought to reach the Indian Ocean by forming a line from the Baltic Sea through the Straits, and continuing to the Gulf of Basra. The British wanted Iraq and Palestine for their oil as well as the Suez Canal, while the French sought control over Lebanon and Syria. The Ottoman Empire decided to strike alliances with the major powers to overcome this dire situation and avoid isolation.

The Ottoman government made its choice when it signed an agreement with the Germans and the Austrians on 2 August 1914. According to this secret agreement, the Ottomans would appear to be neutral until they could mobilize their forces. The day after it was signed, Ottomans declared general mobilization and the Straits were closed to military ships. By 3 August, the First World War had extended to all of Europe.

At the beginning of the war, two German battleships, the Goeben and the Breslau, were in the Mediterranean Sea. They moved up towards the Bosphorus Strait and were allowed to enter on 10 August. However, international treaties prevented the Ottoman Empire from keeping warships in its waters. The Ottomans announced the purchase of the ships from Germany and changed their names to the Yavuz and the Midilli. German soldiers were made to wear the fez.

The Ottoman public was overjoyed by the news, especially because Britain had previously refused to deliver two battleships, the Reşadiye and the Sultan, which had been commissioned and fully paid for by the Ottoman government. The commander of the battleships, Admiral Souchon, was appointed as Commander-in-Chief of the Ottoman Navy. The ships made their way to the Black Sea and bombed Sebastopol and Odessa on 29-30 October. On 2 November, Russia declared war against the Ottomans. The Allied Fleet, consisting of British and French ships, bombed Seddulbahir and Kumkale on 3 November.

On November 5, the British and the French declared war against the Ottomans and the Ottomans declared war against the British, French and Russians on 11 November. The Ottomans were now officially in the First World War.

The Gallipoli Front

Gallipoli was one of the most important campaigns in the First World War. The British and the French embarked on a military campaign in the Gallipoli for several reasons: Taking over the Straits and then Istanbul would allow the British and the French to push the Ottoman Empire out of the war. This in turn would isolate Germany and

Austria-Hungary in Central Europe so that they could encircle them, drastically shortening the war. Furthermore, a timely intervention to control the straits and Istanbul could also preclude the Russians from becoming involved.[4]

On 18 March 1915, the Allied Forces sent the biggest fleet the world had ever seen to cross the Dardanelles. However, they met with extraordinary resistance from the Turkish artillery and were defeated. They had to retreat. Yet this setback did not stop them, since capturing the Straits was essential for their push towards Istanbul. The Allied Forces decided on a land campaign.

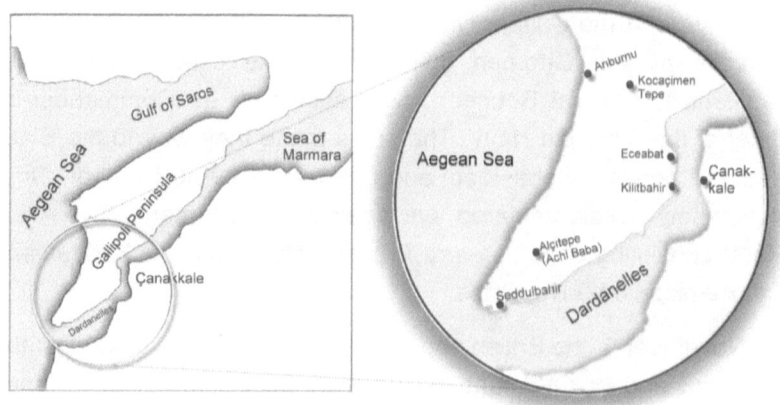

Figure 1: Gallipoli Peninsula

According to the plan, the land campaign would start with landings at Seddulbahir and at Arıburnu, 25 kilometres to the north. The aim was to move inwards from both landing points and take over critical hilltops such as Alçıtepe and Kocaçimen on the first day. The ultimate objective was to conquer the Kilitbahir Plateau. Conquering Kilitbahir would give control of the south part of Gallipoli to the Allied Forces, silence the Turkish artillery batteries along the coast, and allow the

Allied Navy safe passage through the Dardanelles.

The Turkish defenders faced major challenges. They were not sure where the Allied Forces would strike, and the coastline was too long to defend with the very limited resources they had available. Given the limitations, their plan was to keep weaker troops along the coastline and stronger troops as reserves in the back. When the enemy attacked, the troops on the coast were to gain time, while the stronger reserve troops would be mobilized to back them up.

In the early morning hours of 25 April 1915, after heavy naval artillery fire, the Mediterranean Expeditionary Force started landing its main forces in Seddulbahir, along with a smaller force in Arıburnu. To confuse the Turks and to prevent them from mobilizing their reserves, diversionary landings were made at three points at Beşige, Saros and Kumkale.

The Turkish 26th Regiment succeeded in resisting a much superior force that day, and stopped the advance of the Allies. In Arıburnu, on the other hand, the Allied troops managed to move inwards without much resistance. However, Lt. Colonel Mustafa Kemal (Atatürk), who was the commander of the 19th Division in reserve, took the initiative to move his 57th Regiment towards Arıburnu. With the support of the 27th Regiment, he succeeded in stopping the advance of the Allied troops. This was a major blow to the first day plans of the Allies.

The coming days and weeks witnessed numerous intensive clashes in the Gallipoli peninsula. Up to the end of July, when the 42nd Regiment arrived in Kerevizdere, clashes in places like Kirte, Zığındere and Kerevizdere cost thousands of lives on both sides.

Kerevizdere Battles

Kerevizdere was an important target for the Allied Forces. They had to take Kerevizdere to take full control over the Alçıtepe Hill. The

42nd Regiment

Mediterranean Expeditionary Forces, under the command of General Sir Ian Hamilton, had assigned Seddulbahir to the French Expeditionary Corps of the Orient (Corps Expéditionnaire d'Orient - C.E.O.) and the British 8th Corps (see Figure 2). Responsibility for the line from the Kanlıdere River to the point where the Kerevizdere River reached the sea was given to the French C.E.O. Before the 42nd Regiment arrived at the trenches at Kerevizdere, two critical battles took place in this area.

The First Battle of Kerevizdere

Although the Allies were very keen on taking control of Alçıtepe, when the attacks from the flanks did not yield the desired result, the Anglo-French commanders decided to carry out two separate offensives with intensive artillery support. The aim was to seize the Turkish trenches on the flanks and then to launch a joint offensive from both sides to gain control of the area in between. The French C.E.O., under the command of General Gouraud, was to take control of the hills of Kerevizdere as well as Kemalbey Hill.

The area that the French wanted to attack was the responsibility of the Turkish 2nd Division.[5] The 2nd Division had joined the night offensive the day it had arrived at Arıburnu from Istanbul on 19 May, and lost half of its soldiers. It was then reinforced and assigned to the Seddulbahir area.[6]

On 19 June, the French initiated sudden and very heavy shelling of the 2nd Division lines and beyond. With increasing intensity and support from naval artillery, the bombardment continued until the morning of 21 June, leaving the Turkish trenches completely wrecked.

The French attack came at 4:30 am on the same day and most clashes along this narrow strip of land were face-to-face with bayonets. They continued for two days, with trenches changing hands more than once. After two days of fighting, the French succeeded in capturing the Kemalbey Hill and a strip of 200 meters in the trenches, which was far less than what they had planned for.[7]

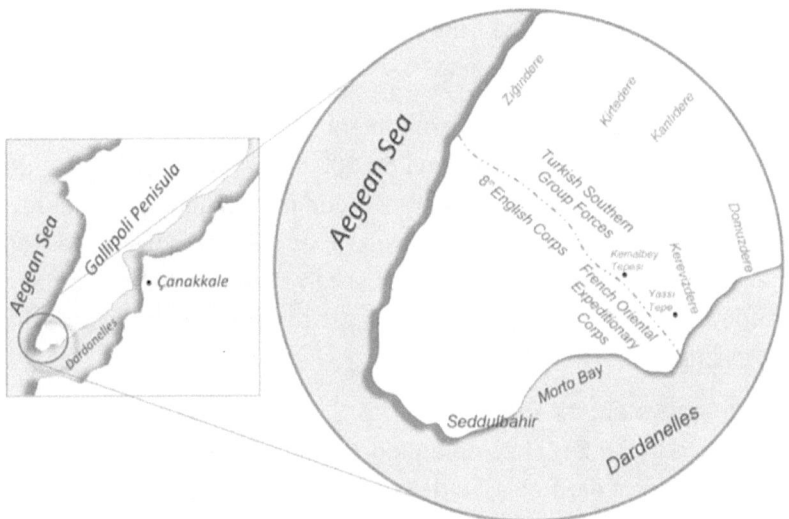

Figure 2: The position of the French and British troops opposing the Turkish forces in Seddulbahir

In the First Battle of Kerevizdere, the Turkish side lost 5,800 men and 79 officers. According to their count, the French lost 2,500 men while Turkish observers reported 7,000 French casualties.[8]

The Turkish 2nd Division lost 60% of its men and was pulled back to be replaced by the 12th Division.[9]

The Second Battle of Kerevizdere

Following their success at the Zığındere Battles, the Allies made new plans to advance their right flank and move closer to Alçıtepe.

42nd Regiment

Accordingly, the French C.E.O. would support a British offensive while simultaneously attacking the Turkish trenches on the southern side of Kerevizdere. General Gouraud, the Commander of the French C.E.O., was wounded on 30 June[i] and General Bailloud, the commander of the 2nd Division, was assigned to his position as acting commander. The offensive was to start at Kanlıdere and extend up to Yassıtepe Hill[ii]. The Turkish trenches were being defended by the 7th, 4th and 6th Divisions.

The Allies began a heavy bombardment in the early hours of 12 July. In three hours, they used around 60,000 shells of various sizes, demolishing the Turkish front line, communication and reserve trenches. The offensive that followed met staunch resistance from the Turkish side. After two days of tough clashes, the French succeeded in capturing a position on Kemalbey Hill, overlooking Kerevizdere.

The most violent clashes during the Second Battle of Kerevizdere took place in the trenches defended by the 4th Division. The French seized some of the front-line defence trenches, but this did not lead to major changes in the main trenches.[10]

The losses incurred by the 4th, 6th and 7th Divisions on the Turkish side amounted to 9,462 soldiers,[11] while the Allies lost 3,900

---

[i] On 30 June 1915, **General Gouraud**, who had left the command post to visit the field hospital, was severely wounded when a shell thrown by Turkish batteries landed very close to him. (*Birinci Dünya Savaşı'nda Çanakkale Cephesi [Gallipoli Front in WW1]*, Vol 5, Book 3, p.173).
According to Dr Vassal's account: *"The General was blown over a wall of ashlar about two metres high and over a fig tree almost into the interior of the field hospital of the 2nd Division. (...) The General had his elbow bruised, his thigh broken, his leg broken. They picked him up fainting in the court of the field hospital. The fig tree had broken his fall."* (Vassal, *Uncensored Letters from the Dardanelles*, p. 149).

[ii] **Yassıtepe**; referred to as *"Rognon"* by the French.

soldiers.[12]

The Suvla Campaign

Failure to achieve the desired progress led Ian Hamilton, Commander of the Allied Forces, to plan a new attack from scratch. Hamilton had become convinced that Seddulbahir was not the right place to attack the Turks, but he kept his new plans secret, even from those closest to him.

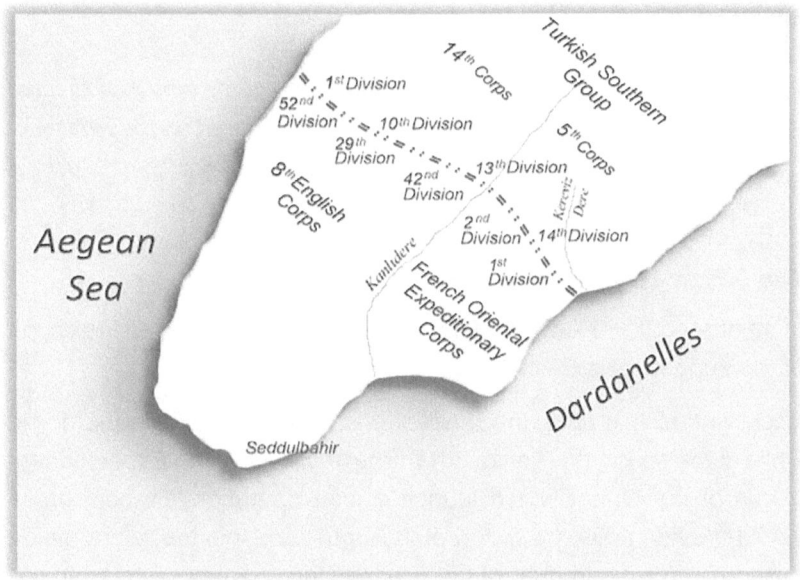

Figure 3: The position of the Turkish and Allied forces in the Seddulbahir area

His new plan entailed a massive landing at the Suvla Port, with troops moving in towards Anafartalar. The landing would be supported by a major offensive from Arıburnu towards Conkbayırı, along with another one from Seddulbahir in the south, while a small detachment would conduct a diversionary landing in Saros.[13]

Intelligence on Turkish forces

In a secret letter sent by the Headquarters of the Mediterranean Expeditionary Force to its corps, the Turkish forces in the Gallipoli Peninsula were estimated to number around 100,000 soldiers. According to the same letter, 27,000 men were estimated to be stationed in the north and 36,000 in the south, with an additional 27,000 in reserve. Intelligence also suggested that 12,000 men were on the Asian side of the Dardanelles Strait, while 45,000 men were stationed in Keşan. The report went on to say: [14]

> *"All reports tend to show that though the enemy may be expected to fight well in trenches, their morale has suffered considerably because of their recent heavy casualties, and that their stock of ammunition is low."*

The French role in General Hamilton's plans

In an order dated 3 August 1915, General Hamilton defined the scope of the support he expected from the French forces.

According to this plan, the main offensive would be from the north, while in the south, the British 8th Corps and the French Expeditionary Corps of the Orient would launch a joint operation. French forces would provide artillery support on 6 August and join the operation on 7 August. The main duty of the French Corps would be to keep the Turkish forces locked in at their front lines and to support the advance of the British 8th Corps, while capturing as many Turkish trenches as possible. This was to enable French forces to gain new territory and ultimately meet with the advancing British 8th Corps to their right.[15]

The position of the forces in Seddulbahir on 1 August 1915

In early August, the South Group of the Turkish 5th Army consisted of the 14th Corps (1st and 10th Divisions) and the 5th Corps (13th and 14th Divisions) (see Figure 3).

From the east to the west, the Allied Forces in Seddulbahir consisted of the French Expeditionary Corps of the Orient (1st and 2nd Divisions) and the British 8th Corps (42nd, 29th and 52nd Divisions).

The Situation in the Kerevizdere valley

The trenches in the Kerevizdere valley were defended by the Turkish 14th Division, which had taken control over the area from the 4th Division[16] on 23 July.[17] The area extended from the point where the Kerevizdere River reached the sea up to Asımefendi Hill (Figure 4).

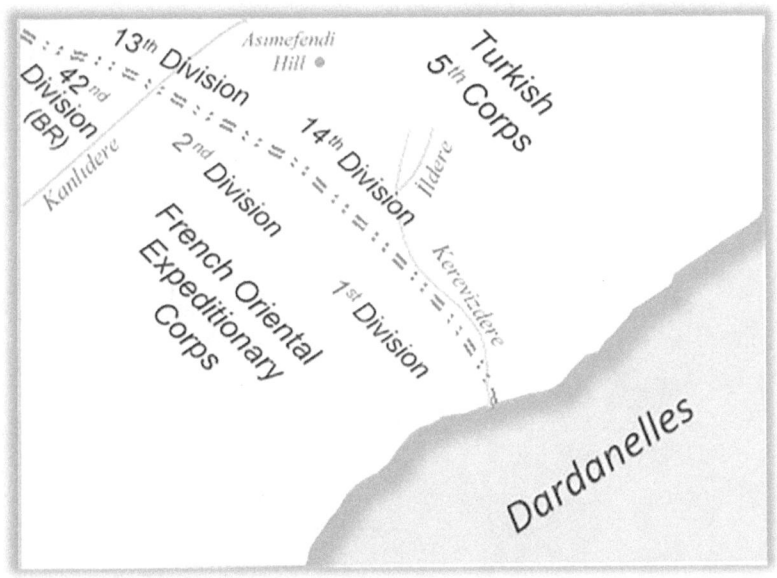

Figure 4: The position of the Turkish Division and the French Corps

The 13th Division was positioned to the right of the 14th Division, while the French C.E.O. was opposite them.

42ⁿᵈ Regiment

The French troops were stationed in an area that was 2,500 meters long, stretching from the coastline to Kanlıdere. The 1st Division stood on the right and the 2nd Division was on the left.[18] To the left of the French forces was the British 42nd Division.

As shown in Figure 4, the majority of the front lines covered by the French forces - 2,000 of 2,800 meters[19] - were being defended by the Turkish 14th Division. This essentially meant that there was only one Turkish division opposing two French divisions.

Part 2

The 42nd Regiment in the Front-Line Trenches

The Regiment arrives in Gallipoli

Prior to Gallipoli, the 42nd Regiment was stationed along the coastline stretching from the Bosphorus strait to Şile. Its main task was to detect and stop any Russian military action in the Black Sea, since Russia was a major threat for Istanbul and the Istanbul strait.[20]

The Regiment had come to Şile and relieved the 41st Regiment on 16 June 1915. In Şile, the Regiment was given a mountain gun and machine gun company.[21] The commander of the 42nd Regiment was Major Ahmet Nuri Bey[I].

A few days later, commander of the 14th Division Lieutenant Colonel Kâzım Bey[II] ordered the Manisa Gendarmerie Battalion to also join

---

[I] **Ahmet Nuri Bey (Brig. General Ahmet Nuri DİRİKER)**, see Biographies, p.151.
[II] **Kâzım Bey (Lt. General Kâzım KARABEKİR)**

the 42nd Regiment. The 42nd Regiment now had four battalions.[22]

After Şile, the 42nd Regiment was sent to Gallipoli, which it finally reached after arriving first in Izmit, then going by train to Uzunköprü and by road to Keşan.[23] It joined the part of the Saros Group under the command of the 5th Army, and was stationed in the Saros coast between Kocaçeşme and Cemilbey Fountain.[24] Its mission was to conduct reconnaissance and defend the coast from a potential enemy landing in Saros.[I]

On 24 July 1915, the Regiment was transferred from the Saros Group to the peninsula.[25] Upon receiving an order from the Saros Group Command, the battalions of the 42nd Regiment gave up their positions to the 17th Regiment and left Saros separately to later meet in Soğanlıdere.[26] Thus, the Regiment became a part of the South Group, forming the reserve of the 14th Division.

The other regiments in the 14th Division were the 41st and 55th Infantry Regiments, as well as the 14th Artillery Regiment.[27]

The 14th Division reported to the 5th Corps under the South Group of the 5th Army.

The Commander of the 5th Army was General Liman von Sanders,

[I] **Deputy Commander-in-Chief (General) Enver Pasha**, in a telegram sent to **Liman von Sanders**, Commander of the 5th Army, on 17 July 1915, warned of a potential enemy landing at Saros. At that time, **Liman von Sanders** did not share his opinion. He was convinced the enemy would attack Seddulbahir. Commander of the Northern Group (General) **Esat Pasha** and commander of the Southern Group (General) **Vehip Pasha**, on the other hand, believed the enemy would attack Arıburnu and head for the Conkbayırı-Kocaçimen plateau. By July 1915, based on various sources of intelligence and the views of the group commanders, **Liman von Sanders** was also convinced that the operation would target either Saros or Arıburnu *(Birinci Dünya Harbinde Türk Harbi [The Turkish War in WW1]*, Vol 5, Book 3, p.265, 269, 272).

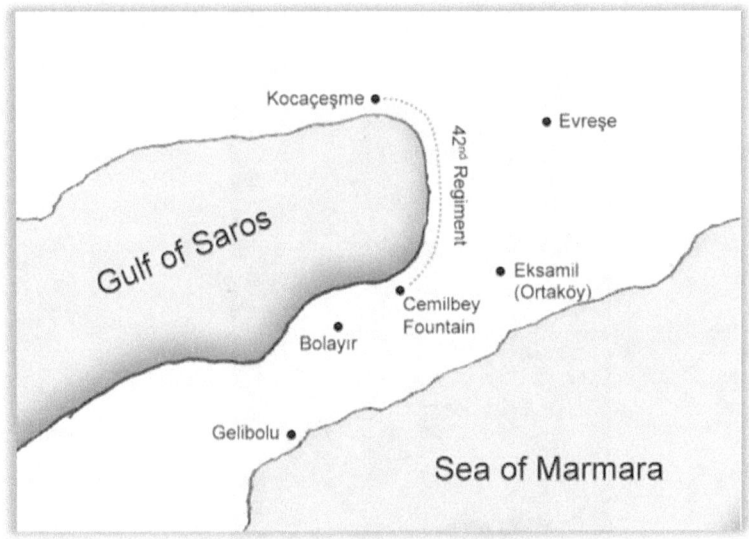

Figure 5: The position of the 42nd Regiment in Saros

while General Vehip Pasha commanded the South Group and General Fevzi Pasha commanded the 5th Corps.

The 42nd Regiment goes to the front line

On 1 August, Lt. Colonel Kâzım Bey ordered the 42nd Regiment to replace the forces at the front line with three battalions.[28] The 42nd Regiment was to take over the trenches that were being defended by the 41st and 55th Regiments[(I)].[29] By the same order, Major Ahmet Nuri Bey became the commander of the front line. Ahmet Nuri Bey

---

[I] Prior to the change, the left flank of the 14th Division's front line was defended by the 1st and 2nd Battalions of the 41st Regiment, and the right flank by the 1st and 2nd Battalions of the 55th Regiment. After the change, the front line, starting from the left (the seaside) to the right, was defended by the 1st, 2nd and 3rd Battalions of the 42nd Regiment along with the 3rd Battalion of the 41st Regiment.

42nd Regiment

Picture 1: Major Ahmet Nuri Bey, Commander of the 42nd Regiment [i]

announced this development to his regiment with the following notice:[30]

> "... An order has been received from the Division concerning the deployment of three battalions of our regiment to the front line and a fourth battalion to the second line. As I will be making some oral announcements regarding the order, commanders and officers of the battalions together are to meet at the regiment command post at 2 pm tomorrow."

That same day, Lt. Colonel Kâzım Bey gave oral orders to Major Ahmet Nuri Bey in his headquarters at Soğanlıdere and placed the

---

[i] Photograph is from the author's family album.

40th Machine Gun Company under his command for deployment to the front line.[31]

On 3 August, Ahmet Nuri Bey gathered his officers and made some announcements concerning the regiment and the current position of the enemy, giving details on how to respond to a potential operation.[32] Changing troops on the front line under constant artillery fire was not an easy task.

In order to facilitate the process, an advance guard consisting of officers and soldiers was sent to the front line that evening.[33] All preparations to move the 42nd Regiment to the front line were completed the next day.

The regiment gathered in the Soğanlıdere square right before the move.[34] In the war diary, Ahmet Nuri Bey recounts these moments as follows:[35]

> "One hour before noon, the officers and soldiers of the battalions gathered at the square in Soğanlıdere and raised the regiment flag. I gave a talk on the state of affairs. The mufti of the regiment prayed for the victory and success of the regiment. Following the sunset, the remaining battalions departed from Soğanlı[dere] to man the front line, which the First and Second battalions had already done the night before. At 7 pm, the command post of the regiment was also transferred from Soğanlı[dere] to the 55th Regiment's command post in Kerevizdere. Intensive artillery, gunfire and bombardment from enemy trenches continued throughout the night."

A few hours after their departure from Soğanlıdere, the battalions reached the Kerevizdere front line. From 2:30 am to 3 am on 5

42ⁿᵈ Regiment

August, the 1st Battalion, led by Major Tevfik Bey⁽¹⁾, took over the trenches, covering 500 meters in length, from the 1st Battalion of the 41st Regiment. Tevfik Bey positioned three companies of the battalion along the front line, and one company in reserve 50 meters behind it.³⁶

Picture 2: Officers of the 42nd Regiment at the Gallipoli Front ⁽ᴵᴵ⁾.

At 2 am on the same day, the 2nd Battalion, led by Major Ahmet Süreyya Bey⁽ᴵᴵᴵ⁾, took over the front line from the 2nd Battalion of the 41st Regiment. Three companies were placed in the front and one company was kept in reserve at the back. The battalion was responsible for defending around 230 meters of the trenches, and its distance to the French trenches ranged from 30 to 70 meters.³⁷ (See

---

[I] **Mehmet Tevfik Bey,** see Biographies p. 153.
[II] Photograph is from the author's family album.
[III] **Ahmet Süreyya Bey**, see Biographies p. 152.

Figure 6 and 7).

The 40th Machine Gun Company under the command of Captain Rıza Bey, which was assigned to the 42nd Regiment, also arrived at the front line.[38] It placed one of its four machine guns in the 7th Company's zone, targeting the area where Kerevizdere met the sea.[39] The other two machine guns, of which one was planned for the zone of the 4th Company to pound Kansızdere[i] and the other for the zone of the 2nd Company, could not be positioned for lack of trenches in the area.[40] The fourth machine gun was kept in reserve at the back.[41] Enemy artillery, gun and shell fire continued until the morning.[42]

It was time for the 3rd Battalion to take over the trenches on the right side from the 55th Regiment[ii]. Once again, an advance guard preceded the battalion. Consisting of four platoons, the advance guard was responsible for getting to know the area and showing the way to the battalion as it made its way to the front line the next day.[43]

The advance guard was led by Captain Şevket Efendi from the 42nd Regiment, and it arrived with 69 men to the trenches defended by the 8th Company of the 55th Regiment.[44]

Another platoon from the 12th Company of the 3rd Battalion, led by Rasim Efendi, arrived at the trenches guarded by the 7th Company of the 55th Regiment. The company commander found a place for the incoming platoon in the existing trenches.[45] Another platoon of 64 men from the 42th Regiment, commanded by Lt. Fahri Efendi, was placed under the command of the 55th Regiment.[46] On the same day, Ahmet Nuri Bey inspected the area taken over by his regiment and reported to the 14th Division the dire need for sandboxes

---

[i] **Kansızdere**; referred to as *"Ravin de la Mort"* by the French
[ii] The other battalion which would take over from the 55th Regiment was the 3rd Battalion of the 41st Regiment.

42nd Regiment

in the main and communication trenches.⁴⁷ He also asked for engineers and sufficient wood and sandboxes to prepare the trenches for the two machine guns that could not be installed before.⁴⁸

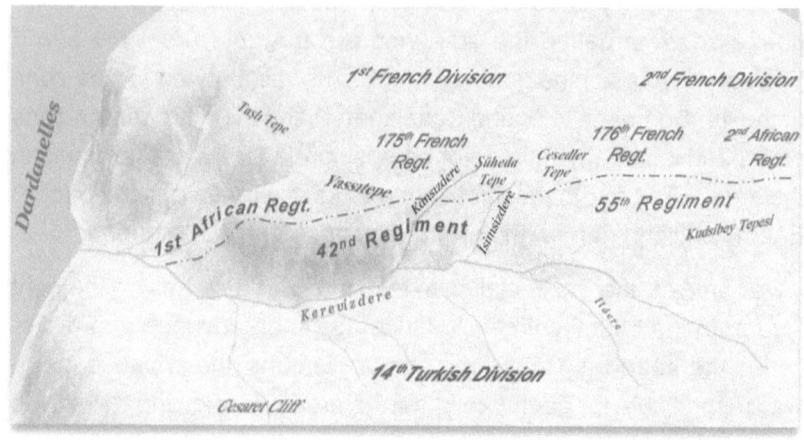

Figure 6: The position of Turkish and French troops in Kerevizdere [I]

The position of the French forces

General Bailloud was in command of the French Expeditionary Corps of the Orient. Bailloud was actually the commander of the 2nd Division, but when General Gouraud was wounded, he was appointed as acting commander. The 1st Division[II] - one of the two

---

[I] These three-dimensional representations aim to give an idea of the general layout of the area. They are approximations based on *Çanakkale Tahkimat Haritası (Fortification Map of the Dardanelles)* by **Mehmet Şevki Pasha** and maps in war diaries.

[II] The composition of the 1st and 2nd Divisions were as follows: 1st Division: 1st Metropolitan Brigade (175th Regiment, 1st African Regiment, Legion Battalion with

divisions that made up the C.E.O. - was commanded by General Schwartz, and held the area from the sea to the point where the Kerevizdere River met the Ildere River. The 2nd Division was positioned to its left and was responsible for the area that extended up to Kanlıdere (see Figure 4). General Simonin was the acting division commander.

In the evening of 2 August, the 1st Division was replaced by the 175th Regiment and the 1st African Regiment. The 1st African Regiment became responsible for the area extending from the coast to Yassıtepe Hill, and the 175th Regiment covered the area from Yassıtepe to the Ildere River.[49]

The 176th Regiment and 2nd African Regiment of the 2nd Division, were positioned to the left of the French trenches (see Figure 6).

The French operation plans

In a letter sent to the 1st and 2nd French Divisions dated 5 August 1915, General Bailloud describes the operation plan and the role of the French Forces.[(I)] Accordingly, the C.E.O. did not have a specific role on 6 August, the first day of the operation. It was to take action on the second day.[50]

The 1st French Division was to attack the Turkish trenches over Yassıtepe and İsimsizdere River. At the same time, the 2nd Division on the left would launch simultaneous attacks on two different points.

---

two companies) and 2nd Colonial Brigade (4th and 6th Colonial Regiments); 2nd Division: 3rd Metropolitan Brigade (176th Regiment and 2nd African Regiment) and 4th Colonial Brigade (7th and 8th Colonial Regiments) (*Birinci Dünya Harbi'nde Türk Harbi*, Vol, 5. Book 3, p.302).

[I] For **General Bailloud's** order no. 905M on the operation plans for 6 August and beyond, see Document 13, p.148.

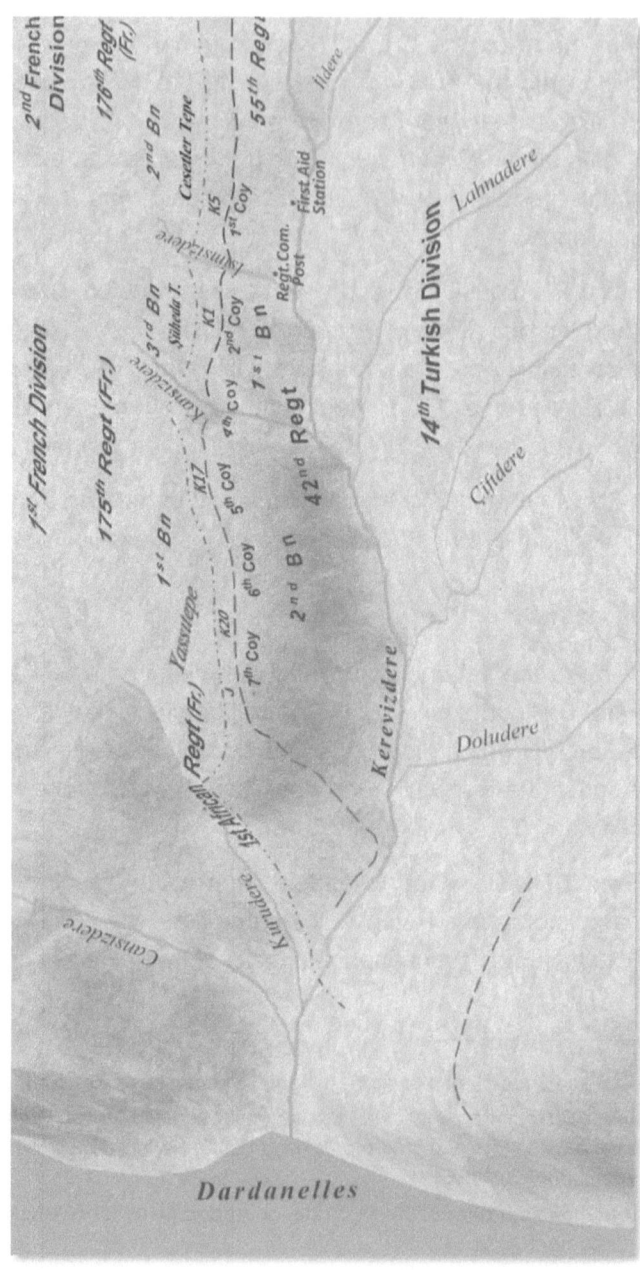

Figure 7: The position of the 42nd Regiment battalions and companies in Kerevizdere Ravine.

Marking of the trenches

The distance between the trenches defended by the 42nd Regiment and the French C.E.O. ranged from 20 to 70 meters. In the Turkish diagrams and maps, the front-line trenches were separated into zones, while the French used alphanumerical markings for both their and the Turkish trenches (see Figure 8).

The clashes intensify

In the afternoon of 5 August 1915, the French intensified their artillery fire and shelling. While the 2nd Battalion did not suffer any casualties, two soldiers in the reserve force died and 15 were wounded by mortar.[51]

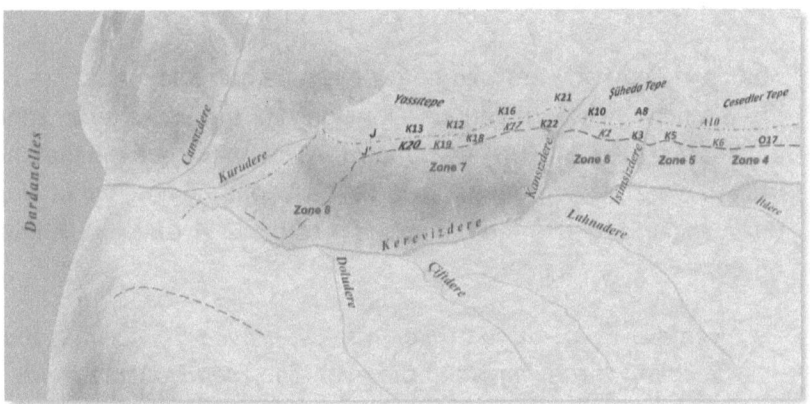

Figure 8: Trench markings (For original maps, see Document 5, p.140; Document 9, p.144 and Document 14, p.149).

Major Ahmet Süreyya Bey reported this incident as follows:[52]

> "According to the information I received an hour ago from Şevket Efendi's platoon, which I had sent to the left flanks, there is no enemy action towards that area, and although they are

throwing mortar everywhere out of fear, until now they have not had the courage to launch forward."

On the right side, guarded by the 1st Battalion, two men had died and four were wounded. French mortars had demolished parts of the trenches, and three soldiers were removed from under the rubble.[53] Gunfire between the two sides continued.[54]

The British attack Seddulbahir; the French wait

On Friday, August 6, General Ian Hamilton's operation plan was put into effect. The British would start the offensive and the French C.E.O. was only expected to support the British with their artillery fire. The Turks were expecting an attack,[55] but they were not sure when and where it would be.

The day began at 7 am with heavy machine gun and mortar fire by the French, inflicting serious damage on the Yassıtepe zone defended by the 2nd Turkish Battalion. When news arrived that the French were moving troops towards Yassıtepe, Major Ahmet Nuri Bey sent an order to the commander of the 2nd Battalion Ahmet Süreyya Bey, saying:[56]

> *"A soldier from your battalion has just arrived to inform us that the enemy is moving along the river. The enemy always sends a force there. On the other hand, your forces are sufficient. Respond immediately."*

He also ordered them to ask for a platoon from the reserve battalion[(I)] behind them in case they needed support.[57] The 1st Battalion was

---

[I] 41st Regiment, 3rd Battalion

also put on alert to give support to the 2nd Battalion if needed.[58]

Major Ahmet Süreyya Bey reported that grenade explosions and gunfire were very intensive at his front, saying:[59]

> "I am absolutely not anxious. The morale of the soldiers is high. God's will shall prevail. Our bayonets are ready for the enemy."

At 10 am, the battle was continuing under heavy bombardment and mortar fire from the French.[60]

While the French prepared for an attack over Yassıtepe Hill down towards the trenches of the 2nd Battalion, they also sent their skirmishers towards the trenches of the 1st Battalion. However, they had to retreat when the Turks opened fire. By 3 pm, the artillery and mortar bombardment in Kerevizdere had stopped, and the area was quiet, but gunfire between the trenches continued intermittently.[61]

Commander of the Machine Gun Company Captain Rıza Efendi reported that he had found a location for the two machine guns that were brought in to fire upon Kansızdere but could not be deployed for lack of emplacements. He also added that he needed 70 sandbags:[62]

> "...if, God forbid, we face a critical situation before the sandbags arrive, we will have no choice but to tear down the trenches and fire as a last resort."

While these events were unfolding in Kerevizdere, the British and French artillery, in line with General Hamilton's order, had started shelling the trenches of the 10th and 13th Turkish Divisions between Zığındere and Kanlıdere. The attack was also supported by naval artillery. After intensive fire from 2 to 4 pm, the British attacked the trenches of the 10th Division. They managed to enter the Turkish trenches for the first time, but were then pushed back with a Turkish counterattack.[63]

The news of the British attack and Turkish counterattack had also reached Kerevizdere:[64]

> *The enemy was hitting our area with shells and mortars and aiming its artillery at the trenches of the 10th Division on our right, and this was followed by an attack by its infantry troops. We received news that, with God's help, their attack has been averted.*

However, the Turks were expecting another attack by the British and French either that same day or the next day. Commander of the 42nd Regiment Ahmet Nuri Bey therefore ordered his troops to be on guard for an imminent enemy attack, and to respond forcefully. In addition to hard biscuits, he ordered an extra one-day supply of bread for the soldiers, adding that each battalion had to keep a minimum of 100 boxes of reserve ammunition.[65]

Due to developments in his own zone as well as the heavy artillery and infantry fire targeting the 10th and 13th Divisions, Commander of the 14th Division Kâzım Bey gave orders by phone to delay the relief in place of the 55th Regiment with other troops. This meant that the third battalions of the 41st and 42nd Regiment would not take over the trenches defended by the 55th Regiment, but rather wait at the back.[66] Consequently, as of 6 August, the 42nd Regiment was defending the left flank of the Kerevizdere front line, while the 55th Regiment was defending the right (see Figure 6).

Since the 55th Regiment had to stay at the front line, Ahmet Nuri Bey moved his command post to Isimsizdere where the 41st Regiment had been located before the changeover. He ordered his 2nd Battalion in Yassıtepe as follows:[67]

To the Command of the 2nd Battalion

<u>Kerevizdere</u>

24 July 331 [6 August 1915] 7:15 pm

Keep the soldiers in the trenches to protect them from bombs. It is possible that the enemy will launch an attack from there. Be very alert. We ask God that they attack. The bayonets of the Forty-Second Regiment will always succeed in defeating the cowardly enemy and capturing their first line.

I expect such courageous and determined action from the whole battalion. I am with the First Battalion where the Forty-First Regiment was previously located. I am waiting there for hourly reports from you.

*Commander of the
42nd Regiment
Major Ahmed Nuri*

At 7:40 pm, the French started the usual artillery fire, which kept the communication trenches and rear lines under fire throughout the evening. This made the distribution of food to soldiers very difficult.[68]

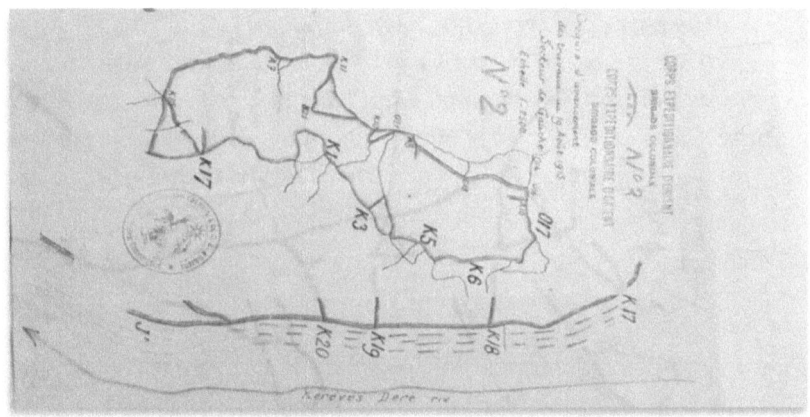

Figure 9: French map[69] showing the front-lines at Yassıtepe

The French attack in Kerevizdere

At 4 am on 7 August, the French took up artillery fire against the Turkish trenches, directing heavy artillery and mortar fire to the rear areas of the Kerevizdere front where the reserve forces were located. Firing continued until 10:30 am, destroying a significant part of the Turkish trenches and watch posts. Turkish artilleries responded by forcefully pummelling the French trenches.[70]

Due to intensive Turkish artillery fire, the French had to retreat to their second line. Ahmet Nuri Bey asked the Division to aim their artillery further ahead because some of the shells were falling too short. However, due to enemy fire, the phone connection with the battalion was disrupted and communication was broken.[71] Hoping that the phone of the 55th Regiment on the right flank was still working, he sent the following order:[72]

To the Command of the 55th Regiment

<u>Kerevizdere</u>   *25 July 331*
                                                     [7 August 1915]

A large part of our zone has been damaged by shelling. (The enemy) is using all its artillery to heavily pound Kerevizdere. Gunfire has not yet begun. I would like to request an update on the situation in the Fifty Fifth Regiment's zone. If your phones are working, please tell the division to fire further ahead.

                                           Commander of the
                                                42nd Regiment
                                             Major Ahmed Nuri

The only remaining way for the Regiment to communicate with the Division was over the phone in the command post of the 55th

Regiment.⁽ˡ⁾ Runners started carrying messages back and forth between the two regiments under fire. The French were increasing the intensity of their fire, which was a sign that they were about to attack. Ahmet Nuri Bey asked for additional ammunition from the second line and ordered the 3rd Battalion of the 41st Regiment, which was waiting in reserve, to reinforce the left flank at Yassıtepe.[73]

To the Command of the 3rd Battalion, 41st Regiment

25 July 331 [7 August 1915]

Regiment 42 Battalion 2 is in an extremely difficult position. Proceed to Kerevizdere immediately in rescue of this battalion.

*Commander of the
42nd Regiment
Major Ahmed Nuri*

As artillery fire continued from both sides, gunfire also began. French artillery caused serious damage along the right-flank trenches of the 42nd Regiment. When artillery fire ceased, the French began their offensive at 10:40 am. Turkish forces responded with heavy gunfire and then met the attackers with bayonets as soldiers poured out of the trenches.[74]

The far-right trenches defended by the 1st and 2nd Company were destroyed and left exposed after the French attacks killed most of the soldiers or left them buried under the rubble. The French seized the opportunity and moved a large force towards these trenches. A platoon led by an officer even managed to reach the trenches of the 2nd Company. They also managed to move one of their machine guns

---

[ˡ] For the positions of the Regiments' command posts, see Fig. 7, p.36 and for the original map, see Document 2, p.137.

behind the Turkish front line via the right flank and positioned it in a way that could keep Kerevizdere valley under flanking fire. The Turks had just moved their reserve forces to the front line and had no other forces left.[75]

If the French were to succeed, they would be able to keep nearly all the Turkish trenches under flanking fire, seriously impairing their defence of the first line. Ahmet Nuri Bey had two options in this very critical moment: he could either withdraw his forces from the area, or launch an attack. He opted for the latter.

The Turkish trenches were hard hit and in disarray. The soldiers had begun to retreat when Ahmet Nuri Bey personally intervened. He took all the men he could find in support functions, and together with these soldiers, launched a counterattack. He described the difficulty of the situation in his own words as follows: [76]

> *The trenches between the 55th Regiment and 42nd Regiment are extremely damaged; all the defenders have either fallen martyr or are under the rubble. The enemy seized the opportunity to move one of its machine guns from the right flank to the rear of the first line, which allowed them to hit Kerevizdere. There were no other troops at hand because the Third Company of the First Battalion had already moved to support the Second and the Fourth Companies.*
>
> *I gave the guns of the fallen soldiers to the unarmed soldiers I saw walking around the Kerevizderesi fountain, as well as to my runners. I fired my revolver towards those who were about to retreat after the enemy attack, and with a force equivalent to a couple of squads that I had managed to bring together, started fiercely shooting at the enemy who were moving ahead with*

their machine gun. The enemy could not hold, immediately took their machine gun, and retreated to their trenches.

The French pulled back the soldiers who were advancing with the machine gun. The French soldiers who had managed to enter the Turkish trenches, on the other hand, were met with machine gun fire from the 55th Regiment and the 42nd Regiment. The Turks attacked with their remaining forces. These moments are described in the Regiment's war diary as follows: [77]

> *... Furthermore, a force of approximately one platoon, under the command of an officer, entered the trenches of the Second Company. They were completely overpowered and could not hold against the enfilade fire from both the 55th Regiment and the left flanks of the battalion, as well as the bayonets of the newly arrived reserve and support forces.*

The 7th Company of the 55th Regiment was holding the right flank of the area of intensive fighting. The commanding officer of the 7th Company, Osman Efendi, described the clashes as follows; [78]

> *...The left flank of my zone was held by the First Company of the First Battalion of the Forty Second Regiment. A big mortar shell landed right in the middle of this company, leaving unmanned a gap in the trenches about the size of around two squads. Although the enemy made use of this opportunity and succeeded in entering the trenches, my side quickly took action and opened flanking fire, and the enemy was forced to retreat from the area concerned. The enemy suffered major losses in this assault and in front of the trenches of the [7th] Company alone, we counted around eight hundred corpses of enemy soldiers, including one officer.*

42nd Regiment

During the clashes, Major Tevfik Bey, the commanding officer of the 1st Battalion of the 42nd Regiment, was shot in the head and wounded. Ahmet Nuri Bey gave the command of the battalion to Captain Mehmet Ali from the 3rd Battalion:[79]

> *Commander of the Third Battalion Mehmet Ali Efendi*
>
> *Take over command of the First Battalion. Maintain your position. Keep me informed on the situation of the battalion. Commander of the Third Battalion, 41st Regiment Osman Bey is at the rear of the Regiment's middle section.*
>
> *Commander of the*
> *42nd Regiment*
> *Major Ahmed Nuri*

The French attacked the trenches of the 1st Battalion again. As Captain Mehmet Ali observed:[80]

> *To the Command of the 42nd Regiment*
>
> *25.July.331 [7 August 1915]*
>
> *Towards the end of the battle, around two squads of the enemy led by an officer with a revolver approached the left flank trenches of the Second Company and a couple of their soldiers even attempted to jump over the trenches, but were killed by a counterattack from the squad located there, and their officer also died.*
>
> *Commander of the*
> *First Battalion*
> *Captain Mehmet Ali*

The French were also attacking the left flanks, especially the section defended by the 2nd Battalion under the command of Major Ahmet Süreyya Bey. Some French soldiers tried to approach the Turkish trenches but were neutralised. In their second attempt, the French forces sprang from their trenches, but were shot when they were partway across, and never reached the Turkish trenches. In a third attempt, they were neutralised as soon as they left their trenches.[81]

While Major Ahmet Süreyya Bey was giving orders to his men, the soldiers on the left flank launched an attack without waiting for orders. It was impossible to order them to return. Other companies who saw them thought the battalion was launching an offensive and joined the attack. The 5th and 6th Companies managed to enter the French first line.[82] In the words of Major Ahmet Süreyya Bey: [83]

> ... The Commander of the Sixth Company and some of his soldiers entered the first line of the enemy, shot more than three hundred men, including an officer, and captured weapons and the officer's hat, while the acting commander of the Fifth Company Captain İbrahim Efendi succeeded in penetrating the enemy's second line, overpowered many soldiers, including two officers. In the meantime, the enemy said:
>
> - Tell your commander that we will surrender. Our soldiers replied by saying:
>
> - Those who will surrender should raise the bayonets of their guns.
>
> But when the enemy started firing again, it became clear that they were trying to deceive the soldiers and our men retaliated with equally fierce fire...

Lieutenant İbrahim Aziz, acting commander of the 5th Company, reported to Ahmet Nuri Bey that they had entered the enemy's second line. He asked for the 1st Battalion to move forward. Ahmet Nuri Bey issued new orders for İbrahim Aziz Efendi, saying: [84]

> Your conduct is commendable. I will do my best to have you promoted. Consider yourself a company commander. Notify me of the headcount in your Company.

Ahmet Nuri Bey also commended the commander of the 2nd Battalion for his success, while reminding him to reinforce the trenches and to ask for help from Major Osman Bey's[I] battalion[II], which was waiting right behind them.[85]

> To the Command of the 2nd Battalion
>
> 25 July 331 [7 August 1915]
>
> I would like to congratulate you for capturing the enemy positions. Reinforce the trenches accordingly. Position your men to never leave. Use your forces wisely. Many forces are causing losses. If you need help, ask the 3rd Battalion of the 41st Regiment right behind you, and they will support you. I have also written to the battalion command concerned.
>
> Make sure you position the battalion in a way that is protected from all types of enemy fire so that it can remain in those trenches.
>
> Commander of the
> 42nd Regiment
> Major Ahmed Nuri

When the 1st Battalion on the right flank also succeeded in pushing the French back, Ahmet Nuri Bey ordered them to attack and seize

---

[I] **Osman Arif Bey (Colonel ERTÜRK),** see Biographies p.153.
[II] 3rd Battalion of the 41st Regiment.

the first line, and to assist the 2nd Battalion. He also ordered them to position the men in a way that would allow them to return enemy fire and never leave their positions.[86]

Upon orders, Lieutenant Sezai Efendi from the 1st Battalion took a platoon with him, attacked the enemy front, and succeeded in entering the French trenches.[87] However, the French responded by increasing the machine gun fire from the right and left.[88]

Ahmet Nuri Bey reported to Kâzım Bey that they had entered the French trenches and asked for additional forces. Kâzım Bey's response read:[89]

Command of the 42nd Regiment

<u>From the observation post</u>   25 July 331 [7 August 1915]
                                             11.30 am

1- The Third Battalion of the Forty-First Regiment has just been instructed to move to the rear of your regiment's line. They are your reserve.

2- Your Third Battalion with its three companies has taken its position in the left flank of the second line.

3- The left flank of the Fifty-Fifth Regiment will support your right flank in the direction of Kansızdere.

4- I have moved your reserve forward.

5- Reinforce the trenches you seize. Report your losses in weapons and soldiers immediately so that I can supply them.

6- You are being sent bombs, ammunition, and sandbags.

7- God help you. I commend you on your success and send my blessings to the soldiers and officers.

Division Commander
Lieutenant Colonel
Kâzım

42nd Regiment

However, fire from the French side prevented most troops from advancing. Only the 5th Company, under Lt. Ibrahim Aziz's command, had already moved ahead and reached the French second line. İbrahim Aziz did not realise that the other companies had started retreating, and composedly tried to hold his ground for over an hour. When French artillery fire from the front and machine gun fire from the left were combined with machine gun fire from the Turkish side, however, Major Ahmet Süreyya Bey, the commanding officer of the Battalion, ordered him to go back. They brought with them around 30 rifles and a telephone set captured from the French trenches. Ahmet Süreyya Bey described the retreat as follows: [90]

> ...While our forces were advancing, the enemy attacked the left flank with the machine gun they had secretly set in place and the grenade launcher they had positioned to the left of the second line. They cornered us from all sides, with machine gun and infantry rifle fire from the flanks and the back, and bombs from the front. Even though the left flank and our trenches fired back against the enemy invasion, the impact on enemy lines was not significant, and as our losses started to increase, the troops could not hold their ground and were forced to retreat to their trenches.

Following the withdrawal of the 2nd Battalion, the platoon led by Lieutenant Sezai Efendi from the 1st Battalion, which had also managed to enter enemy lines, pulled back as well.[91]

In their trenches, the battalions were ordered to hold their positions and to not retreat even slightly. It was of paramount importance not to let the enemy understand they were retreating.[92]

Major Ahmet Süreyya Bey reported the following regarding the enemy trenches: [93]

The enemy trenches to our front consist of three or four lines. They have excellent communication trenches to move from one trench to another. Each trench has infantry and machine gun posts at the back that allow them to open flanking fire on the enemy. The enemy has many different soldiers who wear blue and red shalwar trousers and red fezzes. They have probably been gathered and recruited from the colonies. Their sole source of bravery is the weapons they have in their hands.

The French artillery was constantly bombarding the zone defended by the 2nd Battalion in particular, which made life very difficult for all the troops. Reserves were required immediately, but they had still not arrived. Both battalions had suffered major losses. The 1st Company of the 1st Battalion had only 37 men left: [94]

To the Command of the Forty-Second Regiment

25 July 331 [7 August 1915]

The latest report indicates that only 37 soldiers are left in the trenches of the First Company of your First Battalion which is adjacent to us, and they have issued a request for reinforcement. We request urgent action and further notice.

Commander of the
55th Regiment
Major Hasan Tahsin

Due to their losses, both battalions urgently asked for support forces.[95]

The French were firing not only at the front line, but also towards the reserve trenches in the back, making the advance of Osman Bey's reserve battalion very difficult. There were no communication trenches that led to the front line, which meant that the battalion had to move out in the open. This led to many casualties. Osman Bey described the advance of his battalion to the front line as follows;[96]

> *When the enemy attacked the Forty-Second Regiment which was at the front line on 25 July 331 [7 August 1915], their second Battalion suffered major losses, so we were ordered by the Division to advance to the front line and become their reserve. As there were no communication trenches, we had to advance by giving soldiers directions. 250 soldiers fell martyr and were wounded along the way. The enemy fire was very fierce...*

The 12th Company finally made its way to the front line, but the other three companies from Major Osman Bey's battalion had not yet arrived. It was imperative for these troops to be at the front line in order to help counteract a new French assault that could start in the coming hours. Ahmet Nuri Bey asked the Division to send the support forces as soon as possible.[97]

Meanwhile, the French were still fiercely bombing the Turkish trenches along the Kerevizdere River. French aircraft were flying over the area. The troops were in dire need of ammunition. Major Ahmet Nuri Bey asked the 14th Division to deploy its artillery to counteract enemy shelling and to send soldiers from the medical section to help lift the many dead and wounded from the trenches. Ahmet Nuri Bey preferred to send the newly arrived 12th Company in support of the 1st Battalion, which had been greatly reduced in size during the bombardment and assault in the morning.[98]

The French continued to bombard Yassıtepe. The commander of the 2nd Battalion in charge of this area was Ahmet Süreyya Bey, and he reported that, in addition to their previous casualties, ten more men had lost their lives and fifteen were wounded by enemy hand grenades, which had destroyed the left flank.[99]

To support the 2nd Battalion, Ahmet Nuri Bey decided to detach the reserve of the 1st Battalion and reassign it to Yassıtepe.[100]

> To the Command of the First Battalion
>
> 25 July 331 [7 August 1915]
>
> Send the company of the 3rd Battalion of the 41st Regiment, which is located right next to you, to the Second Battalion on the left flank. Rıza Bey should position the machine gun to hit the lines across from the Second Battalion. According to Captain Ahmed Efendi from the First Company, there are 150 men left. Thus, the losses of your battalion are less than those of the Second Battalion. You also have a machine gun at hand so please make do.
>
> Commander of the
42nd Regiment
Major Ahmed Nuri

In his orders to the 2nd Battalion, Ahmet Nuri Bey informed them that the support troops were on their way. He asked them to hold their ground and to never leave their front:[101]

> Do not, by any means, retreat from your trenches; you will be held responsible. If the companies can stand firm until the evening, many battalions will come to their support.

Some hours later when Major Ahmet Süreyya Bey reported again that the support forces for which they had been waiting had not arrived, Ahmet Nuri Bey wrote back:[102]

42nd Regiment

To the Command of the Second Battalion

25 July 331 [7 August 1915]

I have written to you a few times. That company will come to join you now. You probably have seven hundred men in your battalion. That should be enough to defend an area of three hundred steps. Be at ease. Respond boldly to any night raid by the enemy. The moral and material responsibility is huge. I expect your best effort. Engineering troops have been dispatched.

*Commander of the
42nd Regiment
Major Ahmet Nuri*

Meanwhile the commander of the 1st Battalion Captain Mehmet Ali also reported that they had many casualties and that the headcount had dropped to 600 soldiers. He asked for urgent support from the rear trenches. [103]

The 40th Machine Gun Company, deployed to the front line, gave major support to the offensives launched by the Turkish troops, and helped the 5th Company retreat safely from the French second line. [104]

In his report, Captain Rıza Hayrettin Efendi, commander of the Machine Gun Company, wrote: [105]

The three guns under my command have done their duty. They continued to fire on the left flank of the First [and] Second Battalions and in the previous range. We have only one wounded soldier and no other losses.

The French assault had been stopped, but at the cost of serious losses of the 1st and 2nd Battalions. Their headcount was down by almost half. Many officers had lost their lives in action. Captain Halil

Efendi[I] and Lieutenant Ahmet Efendi[II] from the 2nd Battalion were among the casualties. Captain Hakkı Efendi, Müftü Efendi, and Lieutenant Mehmet Ali Efendi, aide-de-camp of the 1st Battalion, were all wounded. Lieutenant Şevki Efendi, who was wounded, lost his life that same day (Picture 4). The main trenches and communication trenches were full of dead and wounded soldiers. Half of the combat force had been lost, and reinforcements were absolutely necessary to counteract a potential French attack. [106]

A support force of merely 60 men had arrived, but this was nowhere near enough. Some of the wounded soldiers had to wait for two days to be sent to the field ambulance. The firing was so intense that medical units could not come to the front line and stretcher-bearers were not able to do their job. The labour company needed to be sent from the rear lines to bury the deceased. On top of it all, the enemy was throwing poison gas from the vicinity of Yassıtepe.[108]

Picture 3: Captain Halil Nafiz [107]

Ahmet Süreyya Bey reported that the commander of the detachment that had come to his help was also wounded, and that he had sent

---

[I] **Captain Halil Nafiz Efendi:** Born in İstanbul, father's name: İbrahim, commander of the 2nd Company of the 1st Battalion of the 42nd Regiment (Sayılır, *Tarihe Sığmayanlar*, p. 167).

[II] **Lieutenant Ahmet Efendi:** Born in Istanbul, father's name: Mustafa, officer in the 2nd Company of the 2nd Battalion of the 42nd Regiment (ibid 286).

all his reserves to the front line:¹⁰⁹

> To the Command of the 42nd Regiment
>
> <u>Kerevizdere</u> 25 July 331 [7 August 1915]
>
> 1- The commander of the incoming detachment and Lieutenant Hüseyin Ağa of the 5th Company are also wounded. A bomb from an airplane has also caused serious damage. I have sent the reserve soldiers to the trenches. May God be with us.
>
> Battalion Commander
> Major Ahmet Süreyya

To make matters worse, grenades thrown by the French to the 7th Company on the left flanks of Yassıtepe killed 7 soldiers and wounded 20 others. A bomb hit the 6th Company, killing 10 and wounding 6 soldiers.¹¹⁰ Major Kudsi Bey[I], commander of the 1st Battalion of the 55th Regiment, lost his life at Gazilertepe Hill[II].¹¹¹

The 10th Company of the 3rd Battalion of the 41st Regiment, which was to come to the front line to provide support, lost so many of its soldiers on the way that only 117 men arrived in the end. They were first assigned to the 1st Battalion, but were then re-assigned to Yassıtepe in anticipation of another French attack.¹¹²

Around 5:30 pm, Major Hasan Bey[III], commander of the 55th Regiment, reported that the French were moving some of their troops

---

[I] **Major Hafız Kudsi Bey**: Born in Kula/Manisa in 1876; father's name: İbrahim (Sayılır, *Tarihe Sığmayanlar*, p. 66).

[II] The name of **Gazilertepe (Hill)**, where Major Kudsi Bey lost his life, was later changed to **Kudsibey Tepesi (Kudsibey Hill)** (*War Diary of the 14th Division*, H11-001-007).

[III] **Major Hasan Tahsin**: See Biographies p.153.

towards the trenches of the 42nd Regiment.[113]

Commander of the 14th Division Kâzım Bey commended the 42nd Regiment for pushing back the enemy attack, and informed them that he had sent forward two more battalions[II] to support them. He added that the French were reinforcing the front across from the 42nd Regiment, and asked them to prepare for all possibilities.

Picture 4: Lt. İbrahim Şevki [I] [114]

He also noted that the 580 enemy corpses in front of the 2nd Battalion of the 55th Regiment were a clear sign of the magnitude of enemy losses.[III][115]

After a full day of battle, the field ambulance was overflowing with corpses and wounded soldiers.[116]

The French fire continued without respite. At around 8 pm, a French

---

[I] **Lieutenant [İbrahim] Şevki Efendi** (Personnel no: 328-61): Born in Denizli. He fell in Seddulbahir on 7 August 1915 while serving in the 1st Company of the 42nd Regiment. (Letter from the Archives Dir. of the Ministry of Defence, dated 2.7.2015).

[II] The 3rd Bat. of the 41st Reg. and the 3rd Bat. of the 42nd Reg.

[III] According to the records of the French C.E.O., French casualties (dead, wounded and missing) in the attack on 7 August 1915 totalled 780, with 241 killed in action (see Document 11, p.146). According to the Turkish records, however, the number of French soldiers killed in action, only across the 55th Regiment, were counted at 580. This number does not include the French casualties at Yassıtepe Hill, where the fiercest battles took place on that day.

42nd Regiment

Figure 10: Turkish map showing the French attack and Turkish counterattack in Kerevizdere on 7 August 1915 (For the whole original map, see Document 2, p.137).

platoon led by an officer attacked the trenches of the 2nd Company, but all were bayoneted and neutralised. Later on, one French soldier from the reconnaissance patrol who tried to approach the trenches of the 1st Company was taken prisoner and sent to the 14th Division.[117]

Ahmet Nuri Bey saw that the number of combatant soldiers had dropped by nearly half, and it was impossible to defend the trenches against a potential enemy attack during the night. He moved the 2nd Battalion, which was located on the left flank (at Yassıtepe), towards Kansızdere and moved Osman Bey's Battalion (the 3rd Battalion of the 41st Regiment) to the vacant area. This meant that there were now three battalions on the front line defended by the 42nd Regiment.[118]

Throughout the night, new support troops made their way to the front line. The first to arrive at around 1:30 am was the 3rd Battalion of the 42nd Regiment. Towards dawn, two other companies of the 3rd Battalion of the 41st Regiment also arrived. [119]

They managed to hold off the French attack, and the French were forced to withdraw that day. The officers and soldiers of the Regiment had put forth a strong resistance, and over half had lost their lives or were wounded. All the roads were full of dead or wounded soldiers. The field ambulance had been under fire the whole day and had not been able to provide the necessary medical assistance. The soldiers in the trenches had not received anything to eat. The French kept the Turkish trenches under intermittent grenade and artillery fire throughout the night, but their night raids were rebuffed.[120]

Opposite the Turkish trenches...

In his report to the French Ministry of War in Paris, General Bailloud wrote: [121]

> ... One out of the four attacks attempted in the French sector succeeded. Two attacks failed due to strong fire from the Turkish artillery. The fourth attack is still underway. The Turks are showing strong resistance. They are tougher and more effective than in previous clashes. Their artillery fire is very precise and effective. For the first time, the Turks deployed barrage fire.

The French war records describe the attack of their 1st Division as follows: [122]

> 7 August: The 1st Division received an attack order on K1, K9 [around İsimsizdere River], and K17 K20 [Yassıtepe]. After preparatory artillery fire that started at 10 am, the 175th Regiment attacked K9, K1, and the K17 K20 line as of 11 am.

42nd Regiment

The attack stopped in front of K9 and returned to the departure line. Continued very fiercely. Led to around 130 casualties on this front. In the afternoon, major Turkish support arrived behind K9; this attack can only be countered with the support of the 2nd Division.

On the K1 front, we captured the right side of the fortification, but due to enfilade fire towards K9, we had to retreat to a more favourable position a few meters behind. Casualties around 190 men.

At K17 K20 [Yassıtepe], the very moment we left our departure line, we encountered a violent Turkish attack on J [right side of Yassıtepe] with a fusillade on the attacking company's front. In the span of a few minutes, around a hundred men were out of action.

Artillery preparation fire was completely insufficient; the mountain gun unit on O3 was destroyed after 12 shots, the revolver cannon collapsed quickly, and the Turks could protect themselves from the very slow Dumezil fire.

At 12 pm, Commander of the 1st Division General Schwartz ordered the commander of the Colonial Brigade to put one of the 6th Colonial's reserve battalions at the disposal of the attacking commander, to be deployed on top of the large ravine.

Until 2 pm, violent hand-to-hand clashes continued in K16 K12 K13 J trenches. The last front was recaptured after being lost momentarily. The line of departure is now firmly under control.

After the attacks of the 2nd Division stopped, we received orders to not attack again but to hold firmly on our fronts.

The battle is slowing down. We are making use of the evening and night to reorganize our position.

Upon the orders of the Commander of the CEO, the 2nd [Battalion] of the 4th Colonial (reserve of the CEO) came to occupy the fall-back line in the east (Amade Trench).

The medical doctor of the 6th Colonial Regiment, Joseph Marguerite Jean Vassal, recounts the events of the same day in a letter to his wife that was later published as a book, with the following words:[123]

Again, one of those days when one considers oneself lucky to be alive. During the last two days, the English have been landing whole divisions at the new points in Gallipoli. We therefore on the right wing made an attack this morning at 11 o'clock.

Huge artillery preparation. But without great result, for the Turks' trenches were too near ours, sometimes they were only 20 meters apart, to allow our guns to play on them. The artillery 'barrage' operated well behind, but that did not prevent the Turks from crowding into their first line trenches. The Turks, 'lacking in munitions', are sending a hail of 'marmites' on us. Our Morto Bay ambulance has been bombarded twice. It was really terrifying.

I took refuge in a hut which contained a sort of alcove in one of its walls. No use. While I was reading my paper there the whole hut was smashed in, and for two or three minutes I did not know what had happened. Luckily, I was partly protected by the excavation itself. A shell had burst five meters above me, on the slope of the hill.

It was earth, and happily not a single piece of shrapnel, which destroyed the hut and covered me. One more shock experienced! In spite of everything, a feeling of optimism prevails, and, above all, a desire to see something fresh happen."

In a letter dated 9 August, he mentions the same attack, saying: [124]

On August 7 there was a general attack while the British were effecting new landings to the north of Gaba Tepe. Our regiment was the first for this attack. The Kereves Dere is a formidable position which has already cost us many lives, and which cannot be taken by a frontal attack. We are waiting for the English, for advancing on the left. They have captured nine machine guns and 600 prisoners. You will know about this better than we do from the London papers.

I told you that I had been half buried in a hut on August 7. I was certain that we had been bombarded by a ship, and that the shell which fell just over us was a naval projectile.

I was right. It came from an insolent Turkish cruiser which had come up quite close to Chanak, and was calmly firing on us quite at its ease, since all our boats are now at Moudros, even on the days when we fight. The English have succeeded in landing their troops at Suvla Bay to the north of Gaba Tepe. Hurrah! There will be something new to record before long!

On August 7, a shell fell on a field hospital, killing two doctors and wounding a third.

In our lines, a Senegalese, a great big fellow, was carrying a sack of grenades on his head when a Turkish sharp-shooter landed a bullet in the middle of it. The whole thing exploded. The black was cut into two, and several other blacks near him were killed or wounded.

Charles Roux, a staff officer of the French C.E.O., was at the Canada hospital ship on 7 August 1915 due to illness. In his memoirs, Charles Roux recounts what he witnessed that day: [125]

> *The artillery fire at Cape Helles was particularly violent on the right, that is to say, on the French front today. Several times throughout the day, the tugboat carried around 150 wounded in total to the 'Canada'. It's a dismal spectacle: the arrival of a whole bunch of bodies torn to pieces, bloody, wounds dressed hastily, sometimes already dead. The worst-off lie on the bridge of the small tug: some of them have only a few hours left to live. [They] are bruised, shaken by fits, waving their hands in the air; some of them are covered with a blanket or have a flag covering their heads: these are the ones who died during the 15 minutes needed to come from Seddulbahir to the Canada. The tugboat takes them back so that they may have their last sleep on the peninsula, like so many of their brothers-in-arms before them.*

The day after the French attack

The anticipated French attack did not materialize that evening.

The next morning, on Sunday, 8 August, the French pounded the trenches of the 42nd Regiment with artillery and grenades from dawn till 11 am. A support force of around 30 men could only carry some of the bodies of dead soldiers from the previous day's fighting. Most bodies could not be removed, and new support troops were asked to come from the rear trenches to remove them.[126]

The bombardment from the previous day had completely demolished the trenches and roads between the 42nd and 55th Regiments. When the French fire abated, all efforts went into removing and burying the bodies of the fallen soldiers. However, it intensified again

42nd Regiment

after 4 pm, this time leading to damage in the left flanks of Yassıtepe where Osman Bey's[i] battalion was positioned. The French also deployed machine guns to fire along the Turkish front.[127]

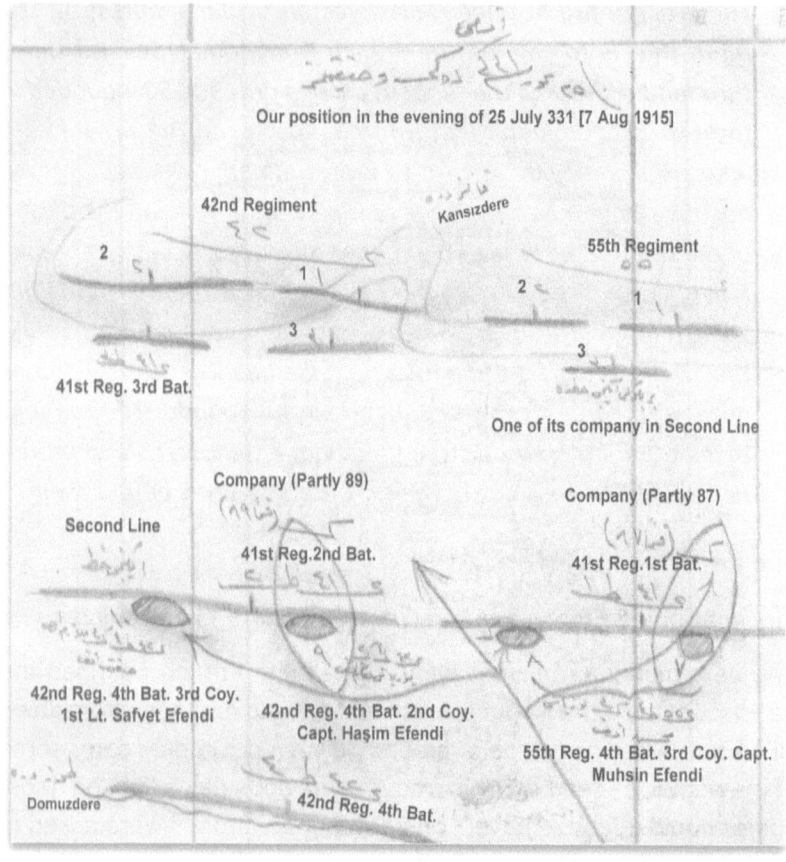

Figure 11: Turkish diagram showing the position of the Turkish forces on the evening of 7 August 1915 (All English translations on the maps from Ottoman are by the author).

---

[i] The 3rd Battalion of the 41st Regiment

To the Command of the 42nd Regiment

26 July 331 [8 August 1915]

Very urgent

The enemy mitrailleuse is trying to hit the sandbags around the observation post to the left of the mitrailleuse near the command post, and they have brought down one. If this post falls, God forbid, it will be impossible to hold our ground in the left flank.

In any case, we urgently request the delivery of one hundred sandbags and the deployment of engineering troops here.

Commander of the
3rd Battalion of the 41st Regiment
Major Osman

Seeing that the French were moving their forces and their machine gun towards Yassıtepe Hill, Ahmet Nuri Bey ordered Captain Rıza Hayreddin, Commander of the Machine Gun Company, to turn two of the guns in that direction and to place one other machine gun in a suitable location nearby.[128]

On the same day, Kâzım Bey sent eight German engineer officers from the Division to the Regiment. Their job was to determine if the French were digging any mines[(I)] towards the Turkish trenches at Yassıtepe, to build mines that could damage the French left flank, and to identify a stronghold at Yassıtepe.[129]

[I] **Mine:** A tunnel that was dug until under the enemy trenches. The aim was to place bombs at the end of the tunnel, detonate them remotely and thereby damage the enemy trenches.

Ahmet Nuri Bey ordered the Battalions defending Yassıtepe to fully assist the German officers. He wanted to be kept updated and asked all troops to be vigilant at all times against an enemy attack, underlining:[131]

Picture 5: *Captain Necati* [I] [130]

> *Our duty here is to defend our positions until we die. It is to disallow any soldier from leaving the trenches we are in. Convey this very clearly to all sergeants and corporals.*

Artillery and gunfire continued throughout the night. The 1st Battalion, which was exhausted from the previous assault, was relieved by the 3rd Battalion at around 7 pm and sent to the reserve trenches.[132]

Commander of the 3rd Battalion Captain Saib[II] reported that no losses had been incurred during the relief in place. He had inspected the battalion and could confirm that the soldiers were all doing their duty. He also added that artillery, mortar and machine gun fire had continued lightly during the night and that they had retaliated.[133]

[I] **Captain Necati:** Personnel no. 315-146, father's name: Hüsnü, born in İzmir. Died on 8 August 1915 while in the service of the 11th Company, 3rd Battalion, 42nd Regiment (Communication from the Archives Directorate of the Ministry of National Defence, dated 2.7.2015). In *Harp Mecmuası (War Journal)*, Captain Necati Efendi is mentioned as belonging to the 46th Regiment. However, the records of the Ministry of National Defence have only one captain named Necati, and the regiment concerned is the 42nd Regiment.

[II] **Ali Saib Bey** (Lt. Col.); see Biographies p.152

Ahmet Nuri Bey reported the situation to Division Commander Lt. Col. Kâzım Bey:[134]

To the Command of the Fourteenth Division,

Kerevizdere

26/27 July 331 [8-9 August 1915]

1- Counterattack to the enemy attack; all of the Second Battalion and the Second Company of the First Battalion took part in the counterattack. All soldiers have been sent to the trenches. Almost all our soldiers were involved in the attack.

2- Although we captured many weapons from the enemy, most were buried under the ground, and some destroyed due to fierce bombardment. Some of the captured weapons could not be carried to our trenches and were left there. The area between the two trenches is filled with weapons and dead bodies. They are almost stacked like piles. Artillery and machine gun fire do not allow us to raise our heads above the trenches. We are only able to do partial observations with the trench periscopes.

3- I had presented the details on the progress of the battle in my report. I was unable to enter exact hours and minutes. Due to the noise of bombs throughout the day and night, it becomes impossible to record events in detail. The area where I am located is targeted by more than hundred bombs every day. As I am unable to receive proper answers to your orders from the battalions due to all this commotion, I too am delayed in reporting to you and truly apologize for this.

4- Many who have fallen martyrs have been left lying in the enemy trenches. In fact, there are some dead bodies from the previous attack between the trenches that have putrefied. It is impossible to say how many.

5- Seventeen pieces of weapons captured from the enemy have been sent today. We will be sending more as we gather the remaining captured weapons that are buried under the ground.

6- None of the officers have failed to fulfill their responsibilities. Whenever possible, I will present to your attention those that can be commended.

7- The number of fallen and wounded soldiers and officers in the First [and] Second Battalions and the Machine Gun [Company] are presented in the attached charts.

8- The enemy trench at the mouth of Kerevizdere, of which I had previously notified you, is being extended towards the existing communication trench.

9- The Third Battalion of the Forty-Second Regiment has taken over the left flank of the Fifty-Fifth Regiment. The First Battalion is waiting as reserve on the hill at its rear.

10- More than three hundred soldiers of the Third Battalion of the 42nd Regiment are assigned to the area of the Fifty-Fifth Regiment.

The 2nd Battalion of the 42nd Regiment is on the south side of Kansızdere and the 3rd Battalion of the 41st Regiment is further south, in the left flanks. I have given orders to the commander of the 3rd Battalion of the 41st Regiment to place a company or a strong squad to the rear left of the front.

This is to present our current situation.

Commander of the
42nd Regiment
Major Ahmed Nuri

Change of commanders on the French side

General Masnou was the commander of the French 1st Division before the 42nd Regiment arrived in Kerevizdere. On 12 July, while in the division headquarters with his officers, he was wounded in the head and knee when a Turkish bomb exploded in the near vicinity. Some of his officers died and others were severely wounded.[135] General Masnou[(I)] was brought to the French ship Bretagne that same evening,[136] but lost his life there on 17 July. Colonel Vimont took the command of the Division.[137] The rear line of the French forces, which was called the C.E.O. line, was subsequently renamed as the Masnou Line.[138]

On 14 July, General Schwartz was appointed as the Commander of the 1st Division.[139] General Schwartz continued until 8 August, when he handed over the command to General Brulard.[140]

On 8 August, the bilateral barrage fire was relentless. The French stepped up their artillery fire to counteract a potential Turkish offensive. They brought in bags full of soil and built parapets to fortify the first line trenches and strengthen them against the Turkish barrage fire.[141]

In his report to the French Ministry of War, General Bailloud mentioned that gunfire had continued throughout the day, but that the anticipated Turkish attack had not taken place.[142]

[I] **General Masnou's** son was a lieutenant and a pilot in the French C.E.O. at Gallipoli. On 18 June, he received orders from **General Masnou** to carry out a reconnaisance flight. He was wounded by Turkish shrapnel and landed his plane with great difficulty (Vassal, *Uncensored Letters from the Dardenelles,* p.135).

42nd Regiment

The bombardment intensifies

The attack both sides expected from the other did not materialize on the 8th and 9th of August. However, the French continued shelling the Turkish trenches round-the-clock both from the land and the sea.[143] Commander of the 10th Company of the 3rd Battalion Captain Mehmet Şükrü Efendi[i] was wounded.

The two reserve battalions were crowded together, and this increased the risk of incurring significant losses. Division Commander Kâzım Bey ordered one of the battalions of the 42nd Regiment[ii] to pull back to the second line[144].

The 3rd Battalion was located to the right of the Regiment now and Osman Bey's battalion was to the left, while the 1st Battalion was at the rear.

Gunfire from the Turkish side continued throughout the night. During the day, the French continued building a 'sap' trench[iii] towards the Turkish trenches. Turkish artillery batteries on the Anatolian side continued to target the French-held shoreline around Seddulbahir.[145]

During the night of 10 August, the French replaced their troops and the 1st Colonial Brigade took over from the 1st Metropolitan Brigade.

---

[i] **Captain Mehmet Şükrü:** Personnel no: 316-292, born in Batum, wounded on 9 August 1915. Died in the Çamburnu Hospital on 13 August 1915 (*Letter from the Ministry of National Defence dated 2.7.2015*).

[ii] 2nd Battalion of the 42 Regiment.

[iii] **Sap:** Small trenches that were dug out towards the enemy lines at roughly ninety degrees to the existing trenches. A new trench line would then be dug at the front of the saps. It was a slow but relatively safe way of moving the trenches forward. Sap-heads were also used as **listening posts** to gather intelligence and follow the action in the enemy trenches.

The 6th Colonial Regiment was positioned on the right and the 4th Colonial Regiment[(I)] on the left.[146]

Meanwhile, the British and Australian forces in the north of the peninsula had failed to progress further. In order to relieve them, the British and French troops in the south were given new orders to keep the Turkish troops tied to their existing locations. Order 942A said:[147]

> *The progress of the main English corps in the North has been slowed down due to the attacks by the Turkish troops coming from Soğandere on the Australian corps. As a result, the Anglo-French forces in the South of the peninsula are working to keep the enemy forces in place with diversionary fire and attacks.*
>
> *The two divisions will be ready to attack soon after receiving orders from the Commander of the C.E.O. The final attack order will be conveyed from the Headquarters to the C.E.O. by 3 pm tomorrow at the latest.*

The same order instructed the French 1st Division to attack K17 and K20 in Yassıtepe as well as K5 in Isimsizdere, and the 2nd Division to attack O12 (Kudsibey Tepe). The French were to open diversionary artillery fire before the main attack.[148]

On 11 August, starting from 1:40 pm, the French gradually increased their artillery fire. When the Turkish troops responded, an artillery battle ensued. The French began to hit the 55th Regiment and the right flanks of the 42nd Regiment. Due to the increasing intensity of the French fire, the Turkish troops started waiting for a new attack.[149] The firing was even more intense than it had been on 7 August, and was

---

[I] On 16 August 1915 the names of the **4th, 6th, 7th and 8th Colonial Regiments** were changed as the **54th, 56th, 57th ve 58th Colonial Regiments** (War Journal of the French C.E.O. p. 229, 26N75/5).

42nd Regiment

directly targeting the front-line trenches.[150]

Major Ahmet Nuri Bey ordered all troops in the first line and the reserve, as well as the machine gun company, to stay alert for a potential assault:[151]

> It is highly likely that the enemy will attack our trenches and those of the 55th Regiment today. If this is the case, keep the enemy under enfilade fire and report your losses frequently.

The trenches to the left of Yassıtepe, under Osman Bey's responsibility, were being bombarded from the sea. Osman Bey reported:[152]

> The enemy has also intermittently held this area under fire since forty-five past one. They targeted the second line trenches and the Kerevizdere. Two enemy warships opened fire. One came as close as the mouth of Kerevizdere but then was beaten back by artillery fire from Eyin Hill, Anatolia, and other locations. Currently there is no reason to expect another enemy attack here. There are no casualties.

At 3:10 pm, commander of the 55th Regiment Major Hasan Tahsin Bey asked Ahmet Nuri Bey to send a company to the first aid station to support him in the event of a likely attack. At 3:40 pm, one of the 42nd Regiment's reserve companies was sent to support them:[153]

> To the Command of the 55th Regiment
>
> 29 July 331 [11 August 1915]
>
> I sent the company you ordered to the first aid station. It is at your disposal.
>
> Commander of the
42nd Regiment
Major Ahmed Nuri

Starting from 4:10 pm, artillery fire began to slow down, and within half an hour, it had stopped entirely. Throughout the night, the French continued with mortar, shell and gunfire, to which the Turks responded with gunfire and hand grenades:[154]

> After this heavy bombardment, the enemy did not dare to launch an attack. However, during the artillery battle, one captain, one lieutenant, and many soldiers were wounded or fell martyr in the trenches.

Artillery fire continued on 12 August and intensified around 3:30 pm. The 13th Turkish Division was getting ready to attack. An artillery duel between the two sides was followed by a successful attack by the 13th Division[(I)]. Infantry and artillery fire decreased after 9 pm and became intermittent.[155]

Solidarity between two regiments

In Kerevizdere, it had not been possible to complete all the communication trenches and middle flanks where reserve soldiers would be located. Before launching an attack, the French would always target the front lines, but they would also keep the rear trenches under intensive fire. Moving the support forces from the second line to the front was therefore particularly risky. That is why an order from the

---

[I] On 7 August 1915, trenches in a small vineyard, just east of Kirteyolu, were taken over by the French. Despite all effort, these trenches could not be taken back. To retake them, the 13th Turkish Division organized a night attack. According to the plan, artillery preparation fire would continue for half an hour starting at 6:30 pm and at 7 pm the attack would commence. The assault took place according to plan and the trenches were recaptured (*Birinci Dünya Savaşı'nda Çanakkale Cephesi, [Gallipoli Front in WW1]* Vol. V, 3rd Book, p.305).

42nd Regiment

14th Division to all the front line regiments said:[156]

> In case of an attack, all regiments currently in the front lines will work with their existing support and reserve forces. Any regiment under less severe enemy attack and fire must help its more hard-pressed neighbour.

After taking over the front line at Kerevizdere, the 42nd Regiment always showed great solidarity with the 55th Regiment in fighting against the French. Ahmet Nuri Bey and Hasan Tahsin Bey showed unwavering support for each other as regiment commanders. In the French attack on 7 August, a shell exploded in the trenches of the 42nd Regiment, killing most of the troops where it landed. When the French launched forward to make use of this defence gap, it was with the help of the 55th Regiment that they were pushed back. That same day, when all the phone lines were destroyed, communication with the Division was sustained through the 55th Regiment.

Similarly, on 11 August, the 42nd Regiment rushed in to help when the 55th Regiment faced intensive fire from the French. The Commander of the 14th Division Kâzım Bey commended the regiments for their exemplary behaviour, saying:[157]

> In the attack on 25 July 331 [7 August 1915], the Fifty-Fifth Regiment guarded the right flanks of the Forty-Second Regiment with its left-flank company as well as its support troops. In a similar manner, during the bombardment on 29 July 331 [11 August 1915] the Forty-Second Regiment ran to support the Fifty-Fifth Regiment with a company. These acts of mutual support are worthy of the highest praise. If such mutual support continues, even if enemy soldiers find an opportunity and succeed in entering, I am fully convinced that they will eventually be bayoneted, and the danger will be averted and eliminated.

Part 3

Trench Warfare

War in deadlock

Between 6 and 13 August, the Turkish Southern Group lost 7,510 men in the battles around Seddulbahir; however, they also inflicted similar casualties upon the British and French forces, stopped their attack, and even captured some trenches. The Turks also managed to send troops from Seddulbahir to help the Northern Group.[158]

After days of intensive fighting, both sides retreated to their trenches in Kerevizdere, waiting while building fortifications, repairing trenches, constructing blockhouses[(l)], and digging communication trenches. Both sides were trying to maintain their existing lines rather than advancing. The war in the area was completely deadlocked.

---

[l] **Blockhouse**: A small fortification protruding forward from the trench that acts as a strong point.

42nd Regiment

Artillery batteries at the back continued firing day and night, while intensive infantry fire and hand grenades were exchanged between trenches that were only 20-30 meters apart. Both sides continued to raid each other's trenches with small squads while mine warfare[1] started to gain importance.

---

[1] **Mine warfare:** Consists of digging a tunnel under enemy lines, packing its end chamber with explosives, and then detonating remotely, thereby blowing up a section of the enemy trenches. Such attacks have a long history that goes back to the medieval era, and were taught in the engineering branches of most modern armies. The Prussian Manual of Military Mining dated back to 1866 and the German Army had practiced mining in the field as early as the 1890s. By the end of 1914, mining had already commenced on the Western Front.

Many of the early miners rested on a wooden board and used a specially shaped spade with their feet. The soil was removed by another man using sacks – often carried by miniature trucks.

The smallest of the mines were **'camouflets'** which were designed to intercept and blow in enemy tunnels before they could reach their targets. As mine warfare developed, more sophisticated methods were applied including mechanically driven boring machines, clay-cutters, and coal mining equipment. Electric and hand-held power tools were also tested, but the noise they were likely to cause, in addition to the problems of maintaining power at the end of a long tunnel, ensured that they never entered general service. Manpower continued to be seen as the most reliable.

Listening for enemy activity from surface listening posts or underground galleries became a vital skill in the tunneling war. This began in periods of silence using the naked ear, along with simple measures such as tubes and tins of water whose surface vibrated when diggers were near. Listening sticks were also used. Other devices soon came into play. The 'geophone' worked on the principle of amplifying vibration or magnifying sounds through sensors and earphones. In the most popular British version, the pair of wooden sensors contained mercury trapped between mica discs, and the listener used a stethoscope. Moving the sensors to bring sounds into balance helped to indicate direction.

The trenches of the 55th Regiment were longer than those of the 42nd Regiment, so on 14 August, the Division Command ordered some trenches to be transferred to the 42nd Regiment. The trenches previously defended by the 7th Company of the 55th Regiment were taken over by Şevket Efendi, commander of the 9th Company of the 42nd Regiment.[159]

Raid on the Blockhouse...

The French were trying to destroy the sandbags in the Turkish front

---

It was not only possible to count the footsteps of enemy miners up and down tunnels but, by correlating sounds from different points, to work out exactly where individuals were. Mining Notes provided useful tables of the likely distances that different types of sound traveled underground. Apart from keeping quiet, there were various attempts to stifle underground noise, including soft footwear, blankets hanged to deaden noise, and even rugs or carpeting on tunnel floors. There was a specially designed single-wheel barrow shod with a solid rubber tire. One special trick was the use of dummy picks and shovels, which could be operated at a distance using a cord. Some struck at a surface, thereby misleading the enemy or covering the noise of real activity. Some galleries came very close to enemy lines[*]. For instance, the 181st Tunneling Company was able to hear the enemy at such close quarters that conversation was fully intelligible. For almost three days, an intelligence officer, aided by an interpreter, was able to take notes on German works. The plans of earlier mines appear haphazard and dendritic, almost like the branches of trees. In every tunnel, lighting and ventilation were problems to be confronted. Lighting could be problematic since a naked flame, put together with various forms of gas and explosive, presented a potentially lethal cocktail. Possible solutions included civilian-type miners' lamps and sealed electric lighting. Canaries or mice in cages gave early warning of dangerous concentrations of toxic gases and lack of oxygen (for details, see Bull, *Trench: A History of Trench Warfare on the Western Front*, p. 163-169).

(*) Similar incidents also took place in the Gallipoli Front (see p.124).

line with Nordenfelt guns. The Turkish left flanks around Yassıtepe Hill were trying hard to deal with this problem; [160]

To Regiment 42 Command

5 August 331 [18 August 1915]

The enemy continues to destroy the sandbags with the rifle or large object that I described in my report this morning. Sandbags have been set on fire and subsequently extinguished four times. They make it impossible to place sandbags on the trenches. As the bags are small, they burst with just a single shot. The location of this gun must be along the enemy's right flanks (our left flank). They have built a place with sandbags there. If they manage to elevate the road, they will destroy our mitrailleuse trench. Once open, it will be very difficult to close this gap. It is up to your discretion to have the artillery destroy this location. Our rifles do not penetrate their sandbags.

Commander of the 3rd Battalion of the 41st Regiment
Osman

The place in question was the 'Matillo' blockhouse[(I)] that the French had constructed at the mouth of the Kerevizdere river. This fortification would enable the French to open flanking fire and constituted a major threat for the 42nd Regiment. This part of the front would be

---

[I] **Matillo**: The blockhouse was probably named after Lt. L. François Matillo, from the 4th Colonial Regiment, who was wounded in the Kerevizdere battles on 21 June 1915 and lost his life two days later (*War Journal of the Expeditionary Corps of the Orient*, p.125, 26N75/3; *Le portail de la généalogie en France*, http://memorial-genweb.org/~b1914-1918/resultpatro.php).

host to numerous clashes in the days and weeks ahead. The French had managed to elongate their trenches by 20 meters on the opposite side of the Kerevizdere river. Just before 13 August, they managed to extend it another 15 meters in three days, for a total of 35 meters of new trenches. To prevent the French from working in the area, the Turks launched mortar fire during the whole day on 13 August and dispatched patrol columns at night.[161]

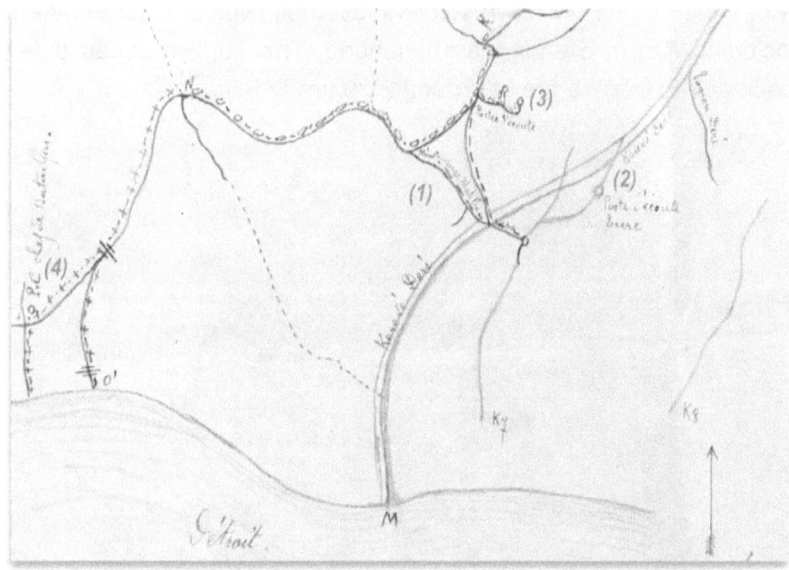

Figure 12: The Matillo blockhouse in a French map[i] (1- Matillo blockhouse, 2- Turkish listening post, 3- French listening post, 4- Command post of the French battalion).

---

[i] For a 3-D representation of the area, see Fig.13. For another original map showing the structures at the mouth of Kerevizdere, see Document 4, p.139.

42nd Regiment

Since the blockhouse was a major threat to the Turkish trenches, the Turks decided to raid the Matillo blockhouse and the French trenches on 18 August 1915. A squad under Lieutenant Rasim Efendi's[I] command, along with another platoon brought in from the second line under First Lieutenant İbrahim Efendi's command, were ordered to carry out the ambush. Just when these troops were about to reach the opposite trenches, the French noticed the attack, opened severe gunfire, and started throwing bombs. Although the Turks responded with firing of their own, two soldiers lost their lives and some others, including Rasim Efendi, were wounded. The Turkish squad pulled back due to intense fire at around 2:30 am.[162]

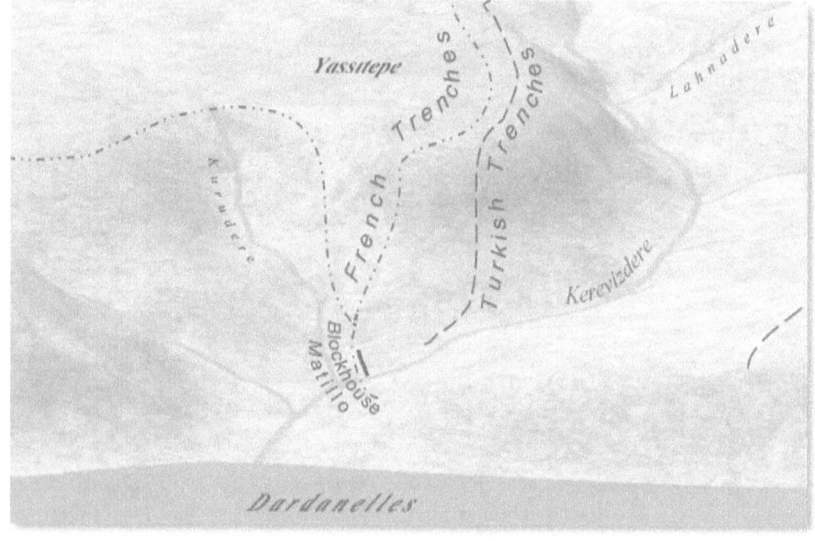

Figure 13: Position of the French blockhouse

[I] **Lt. Rasim** (Personnel no: 331-267): Born in Erzurum, father's name: Mustafa, fell in Kerevizdere on 18/19 August 1915 while serving in the 4th Company, 3rd Battalion, 42nd Regiment (Letter from the Ministry of National Defence, Directorate of Archives, dated 2.7.2015).

Two soldiers who had managed to enter the French line reported that the French trenches were dug quite deep and had proper support trenches. Lieutenant Rasim died shortly afterwards from his severe wounds.[163]

Ahmet Nuri Bey never forgot this young lieutenant, mentioning him in his memoirs written years later:

> *The enemy built a blockhouse close to the mouth of the Kerevizdere. This allowed them to fire from the sides. We tried very hard to counter it but did not succeed.*
> *To carry out a sudden attack, the Division appointed a lieutenant from the regiment called Rasim Efendi. This officer was to approach the blockhouse with his squad during the night and carry out a sudden attack. The enemy learned of Lieutenant Rasim Efendi's move early on. They hindered the attack with shells, machine gunfire, and bombs. Half of the forty-man squad died or was wounded. He himself was wounded. One of the soldiers, who did not want to leave Rasim Efendi in the hands of the foe, carried him five hundred meters to the first-aid station where the officer died. He was an invaluable officer.*

In the end, the operation against the French blockhouse failed. Having succeeded in averting the attack, the French continued to fortify and extend the existing structure. The sounds of engines coming from three different points of the French line were a clear indication that they were busy digging. The French also continued firing with Nordenfelt guns to destroy the sandbags on the Turkish side and to set them on fire with grease-soaked cloths.[164]

In the morning of 19 August, the French Colonial Brigade (54th and 56th Colonial Regiments) was relieved in place by the Metropolitan Brigade (175th Regiment and 1st African Regiment).[165] That same day, the French extended their trenches around the mouth of Kerevizdere even further and reached the Turkish communication trench.[166]

A squad of 40 men led by Lt. İbrahim Efendi was sent to the area at around 9 pm. İbrahim Efendi made half of his men lie down along the communication trench so as to protect his flanks. With the remaining half, he approached the French trenches and attacked suddenly. However, his attempt triggered massive infantry and machine gun fire, as well as bombardment from the new French trenches. When İbrahim Efendi lost 4 men and 10 others were wounded, he had to retreat. The other half of the squad could not move because the French had filled the whole area with searchlight and incendiary projectiles.[167]

Throughout the night, the French fortified the structure with sandbags and barbed wire. If they could turn the place into an artillery or machine gun emplacement, the threat to the Turks would increase substantially.[168]

Commander of the 3rd Battalion Osman Bey reported that the French were about to reach the Turkish communication trench and that it was no longer possible to send forces via the front line. The only remaining option was to launch an attack with forces that could come from the second line. The Turks were throwing mortars to keep the French from working, but to achieve a concrete result, they would have to deploy their patrol columns. In the meantime, both sides relentlessly exchanged artillery and gunfire. The Turks were also using howitzers to damage the trenches that the French had successfully extended to Kansızdere. The French, as usual, were harassing the Turkish front and its rear with intermittent artillery and mortar fire.[169]

Once again, the Turks planned an attack against the increasingly threatening French. The plan was for First Lieutenant Ibrahim and a squad of volunteers from the 2nd Battalion to launch a new offensive. The Division was asked to provide a rapid-firing mountain gun, which would pound the enemy lines and facilitate the execution of the operation. This gun was positioned at the back of Osman Bey's battalion at 2 am on 21 August. It started firing at 3:30 am, launched 41 shots in 15 minutes, and was followed by infantry fire.[170]

However, only 3 or 4 shells landed in the French trenches. Although it was clear that the artillery fire had not succeeded, infantry forces began their offensive. Eight soldiers waiting in the combat emplacements with hand grenades also jumped forward. Clashes soon intensified when the French responded from their trenches along Kerevizdere, deploying their mitrailleuse in Yassıtepe and their artillery in Hisarlık. The squad could not advance too far because the mountain gun did not cause sufficient damage, and the steep and rocky terrain prevented a fast move, exposing the soldiers to heavy gunfire. Four soldiers managed to approach the French lines, but one died right there on the spot when he stepped on a caltrop[(I)] placed by the French and the other three were wounded. Realizing that the attack had no chance of succeeding, the squad withdrew close to dawn.[171]

In the early morning hours, a French war ship and torpedo boat made their way to the shore. The French were afraid that a larger Turkish offensive would follow the move by the squad. Throughout the night, they lit up the whole area by throwing incendiary projectiles while simultaneously pounding the Turkish rear lines. By sunrise, it was

---

[I] **Caltrop:** Also called "crow's foot", is made up of four sharp nails or spines. When placed on the ground, one of the nails always points upward. Caltrops caused serious harm to soldiers who stepped on them.

clear that the Turks had not succeeded, as the only visible damage in the French trenches were two holes. As the day progressed, only the routine exchange of fire continued.[172]

The war diary of the 14th Division depicts the situation on the same day as follows; [173]

> ...Those who carried out the attack report that there are two trenches on the enemy's side with internal passages between them. There are posts and wires on the ground and there are wires, caltrops and posts 30 meters from the trenches. It is impossible for the infantry to enter or to maintain their position. The location is more barren than the Kerevizdere valley. It is at the bottom of the Yassıtepe, Taşlık and Hisarlık hills. The troops of the 6th Division who launched an attack along the valley earlier have all fallen martyrs.
>
> If this trench moves any further towards us, it can start hitting the rear of the first line. Therefore, it is imperative to destroy this trench and to erect high support trenches by sending many sandbags to the first line.

Seeing that the mountain guns were not effective enough, the Turks planned to use heavy howitzers and mortars.

Soldiers who fall asleep out of sheer exhaustion while firing...

Life in the trenches was extremely challenging for the soldiers who had to cope with all kinds of difficulties, including lack of sleep, food and relentless artillery and gunfire.

The report sent by Major Osman Bey to the 42nd Regiment alludes to the immensely difficult conditions;[174]

Gallipoli 1915

To the Command of the 42nd Regiment

From Kerevizdere left flank

5 August year 331 [18 August 1915]

Ever since the soldiers of the Battalion departed from Makriköy and arrived at the first line, they have had no sleep at night whatsoever, aside from two nights. With all the mortar fire, their situation during the day is obvious. We have been in the second line, but given how they have to work there, the soldiers have not had a single night's sleep there either.

I am hoping that this is known to the Distinguished Division Commander. The task is sacred and important. Its importance requires alert and prudent action. The Battalion has lost its most distinguished corporal and soldiers. While the existing composition is as it is, it has been significantly weakened three times by sending soldiers to other units. Under the current circumstances, the numbers have declined and the combatants in the battalions are down to a hundred men. Although it appears like there are five hundred men, when you consider and deduct the unarmed soldiers doing medical and other services, those who have been ordered to rest by doctors, those who have been retained here with light wounds, and those who cannot see during the night, the remaining total is what I have indicated above. This is the reality. If the companies that are currently front-line reserves could take turns with these soldiers, who are dizzy from lack of sleep, these soldiers who have not had a single night of shut-eye since they arrived will have the chance to rest a little and get back to their senses. They are so exhausted that they cannot understand what they are told. [We] even came across soldiers in the patrol column who fell asleep while shooting during the night. Despite checking on the soldiers throughout the night, it is impossible to prevent them from falling asleep. Given the importance of the task, I request that you take into consideration what I have explained. Because the purpose again is to be of service to the country, Sir.

Major Osman
Commander of the 3rd
Battalion, 41st Regiment

Hasan Tahsin Bey

In the morning of 21 August, Commander of the 55th Regiment Hasan Tahsin Bey had inspected his zone and was returning to his post. At 6:30 am, this respected commander was shot in the chest by infantry fire around Gazilertepe Hill. He died from his wounds within five minutes. Under his command, the 55th Regiment had worked in great harmony with the 42nd Regiment. Upon his death, the Commander of the 14th Division Kâzım Bey sent a condolence message to his troops: [175]

> The distinguished commander of the Fifty-Fifth Regiment Hasan Tahsin Bey has fallen martyr. I would like to express my condolences to the Division. Let us postpone our very natural sorrow for his loss until our victory. Let us keep our bayonets even sharper with this martyr's revenge augmenting our already existing feelings of hate and revenge against the enemy. Let us see the loss of these sacred lives as the natural order of events for the time being that will lead us to our victory. Let us not lose our calm and composure. The sacred soul of Hasan Bey is now asking us for fortitude and even more attention and loyalty to our duty. Let us remember him. And, God willing, let us work to take his revenge and defeat the enemy.

Commander of the 3rd Battalion Abdülaziz Efendi was appointed to temporarily replace him.[176] On 23 August, Major Tevfik Bey, who had been wounded in the head on 7 August while commanding the 1st Battalion of the 42nd Regiment, became the new commander of the 55th Regiment.[177]

Osman Bey's battalion retreats

On 22 August, howitzers were deployed to prevent the construction of the French trench that was heading towards the Turkish lines at Kansızdere. The French retaliated by throwing shrapnel bombs, though neither side was effective in their efforts. At around 4:15 pm, the French bombardment started again and lasted for two hours, but did not cause any losses.[178]

Osman Bey's battalion had been defending the trenches at Yassıtepe and was exhausted and depleted. The Division ordered the troops to rest in Soğanlıdere and the 1st Battalion to move from the right flanks to replace them. However, this changeover was not easy and had to be done one company at a time. A Nordenfelt was deployed to damage the sandbags facing the left flank. While the French continued to fire with their guns, artillery and grenades, the Turkish artillery launched 20 howitzers to the French trenches located at the mouth of the Kerevizdere. Nevertheless, they did not inflict the damage they had hoped for, and bilateral fire continued intermittently throughout the day and night.[179]

The Kerevizdere trenches

A significant part of the Turkish trenches at Kerevizdere were located on very difficult terrain. This increased the casualties on the Turkish side.

In one month, from 23 July to 22 August, the 14th Division lost half of its strength: 53 officers (18 killed and 35 wounded) and 4,941 soldiers (1,866 killed and 3,075 wounded). Furthermore, since the reserve troops of the Turkish army were running low, it was possible that the Division would have to remain in the trenches, perhaps until the end of the war. It was necessary to use the resources available with utmost care.[180]

Commander of the Division Kâzım Bey wrote a detailed report to the 5th Corps. Briefly, the report said:[181]

> The front line occupied by the 14th Division has two different characteristics. The northern half of the front[I] has a dominant position over the enemy trenches. The distance between the French trenches and combat emplacements is wide. There are reserve and support areas that have been dug previously. The area and ground are suitable for work. The southern half of the front has a challenging topography[II], with some areas very hard and rocky while others are very loose. The reserve and support emplacements, which should be right behind the combat emplacements, are nothing more than holes dug into rocks on the surrounding steep hills. There are no existing trenches or communication paths like the ones other divisions have found in their areas, and this has been a major obstacle for the 14th Division. Since 23 August, when the Division took over these trenches, only two communication trenches have been completed because of the difficulties posed by the terrain. Therefore, it has not been possible to move the support troops forward from the second line during enemy attacks. During such

---

[I] North of the neck between Bağlıksırt and Hill 83. In other words, north of the meeting point between the Ildere and Kerevizdere rivers (see Fig. 4 and 6).
[II] To get an idea of the challenging nature of the field topography, see Fig. 6 and 7.

an attack on 7 August, one of the battalions sent from the second line took 2 hours to reach the first line, and the second battalion arrived after 5 hours. As it is imperative to have reserve and support emplacements right behind combat emplacements, six battalions had to be kept at this line. There was no other way to mobilize support from the second line in time to counteract a sudden attack. However, there are considerable setbacks in keeping six battalions in and immediately behind the first line. Due to overcrowding in the trenches, the French artillery and gunfire have hit many men and increased casualties. A fortification would have helped to reduce the losses, but the material necessary to make these could not be obtained. As a result, there were very few structures to protect the soldiers and most soldiers were left out in the open. This further increased the loss of life.[182]

Another difficulty is the steep valley going downhill right behind the first line. In case a strong and sudden enemy attack were to require the battalions to evacuate the first line, the battalions would incur significant losses because to retreat, the soldiers would have to first go downhill to reach the riverbed, and then climb uphill again to reach the support trenches. The ground up the hill is loose, and rain and winter weather will further aggravate the problem.[183]

Moreover, the 41st Regiment has been sent to support the Northern Group, making it impossible to replace the exhausted troops in the front line.[(I)] The 55th Regiment, which arrived at the first

---

[I] On 9 August 1915, Commander of the Northern Group Brigadier General **Esat Pasha** asked for support from his brother, the Commander of the Southern Group,

line on July 26, had to stay there for almost a month.[184]

Considering all these factors, one option was to move the front-line trenches forward and another was to pull them behind the support trench under preparation. To move the line forward, the Turks would have to capture the French front line. This in turn required sufficient artillery fire, followed by an attack. Considering that the Division front was 2,000 meters long, and 3 shells would be required for each meter, it would be necessary to deploy 6,000 shells just to prepare for the offensive. Losses to be incurred during the offensive along with those resulting from any potential counter-offensive by enemy forces, would also have to be taken into account.[185]

Pulling the trenches back seemed like the easier choice. However, this would mean losing the structures seized along the front line. The support trench, which was still under construction, had many shortcomings, and it was impossible to use it as a front line. Furthermore, the existing front-line trenches would have to be preserved as outposts for any general offensive planned in the near future. Once evacuated, it would be extremely difficult and costly to cross the Kerevizdere valley again to re-capture these lines.[186]

The 5th Corps, which received this report, wrote back to say that the offensive was postponed due to lack of ammunition and the deployment of one of the Division's regiments to the Northern Group. The

---

Brigadier General **Vehip Pasha** against the new forces that the British would land in Arıburnu. **Vehip Pasha** sent his final two reserves (**41st** and **28th Regiments**) to the Northern Command (*Birinci Dünya Savaşı'nda Çanakkale Cephesi, [Gallipoli Front in WW1]* Vol. V, 3rd Book, p. 343).

existing trenches would be maintained, and the existing roads and trenches would be improved until enough troops and ammunition became available for an attack. Every night, small squads equipped with hand grenades were to attack the French trenches that were getting closer to the Turkish trenches from the left flank[(I)] to show that there was an agile and strong force against them.[187]

An offensive attempt against the French blockhouse...

On 22 August, the Turks formed two squads from infantry and engineering units to stop French activity in the blockhouse and in the trench which they were expanding. Since a full moon was illuminating the environment, the attack was postponed to after midnight.[188]

The attack finally started at 2 am on 23 August. The squads succeeded in approaching the French trenches and in throwing their grenades. However, the French were waiting and retaliated fiercely from their firing slots. They quickly engaged their mountain and machine guns. The Turkish squads came under intense fire and were unable to dig the holes for the dynamite. They blasted the dynamite already in place, but this did not yield any result. After two more hours, the squads retreated back to their trenches at around 4:45 am.[189]

The French attack back...

Having avoided the Turkish attack, the French mobilized a force of 50-60 men led by an officer at around 9 am on that same day. They started advancing along the deserted communication trench in Yassıtepe, across from the 11th and 12th Companies.[190]

[I] Trenches at the mouth of the Kerevizdere river.

42nd Regiment

> To the Command of the 14th Division
>
> 9:00 am
>
> The enemy wants to attack in the direction of the First Battalion. They have jumped out of their trenches. We are retaliating. The phone is cut off. For your information and consideration.
>
> Commander of the
> 42nd Regiment
> Major Ahmed Nuri

The attack was made by a troop from the 1st African Regiment.[191] The fire opened by the Turkish side succeeded in stopping the assault[192] and the situation report said:[193]

> To the Command of the Second Zone
>
> 11 August 331 [24 August 1915] 8:10 pm
>
> Observation Deck
>
> Today, one officer and ten soldiers from the enemy forces who attempted to attack from Yassıtepe were killed. They are lying very close to the bomber's pit of the enemy communication trenches, but our patrol columns will attack those communication trenches tonight and try to seize the epaulets, documents and guns of the dead soldiers.
>
> Commander of the
> 14th Division
> Lt. Col. Kâzım

One of the French mortars fell on the Turkish side of the communication trenches, leading to casualties among the squads located there. This created an opportunity for the French to move their observation post forward. They quickly fortified the new position with sandbags and iron plates. Some of the Turkish artillery fire landed in the French trenches. After a period of calm, the Turkish artillery started battering the trenches in Çatalağaç direction. This was followed by the daily artillery and grenade fire.[194]

It was very important for the Turks to prevent the French from advancing their trenches. A squad from the 42nd Regiment was sent to the area on 24 August but was forced to retreat when fire and shelling from the French side left ten soldiers wounded. Two patrol columns made up of one squad each were sent to trenches at the mouth of the Kerevizdere river. Due to intense fire, they could not approach the French trenches either and continued to fire from their positions.[195]

Bilateral attacks continue

During the same evening, the French tried to destroy the Turkish trenches at Yassıtepe with incendiary projectiles containing melinite but were not successful.[196]

At 3:30 am on 25 August, a Turkish squad attacked the listening post (A25) at Yassıtepe. However, the French were prepared and used their hand grenades effectively to push the Turks back. This was followed by heavy infantry and artillery fire by the French 1st Division. The Turks were quick to respond.[197]

Heavy artillery and mortar fire from the French trenches followed and the Turkish artillery retaliated. At that moment, 20-30 soldiers jumped out of the French trenches and started throwing grenades from the right flanks of the 42nd Regiment to the left flanks of the 55th Regiment. Once again, Turks responded with heavy fire and the French were pushed back. Finally, at 4:20 am, all fire ceased.[198]

At 3:40 pm, wind shear caused a French aircraft with two men aboard that had taken off from Bozcaada to crash into the sea. The French were able to find the aircraft and the dead pilot.[199]

A new attack on the blockhouse

Turkish artillery started shelling the Matillo blockhouse and the bridge at the mouth of the Kerevizdere for two hours starting from 5:30 pm. Although it was limited, artillery shells did cause some damage, destroying parts of the French trenches. A Turkish detachment, consisting of three infantry and engineering squads, prepared for an attack to be launched after the artillery fire ceased. The detachment was equipped with explosives, wire cutters and wire gloves, and was further supported by a squad led by 2nd Lt. Halil Efendi, which arrived just in time from the second line.[200]

The operation started at 1 am on 26 August. The engineers split into two groups. One group headed for the blockhouse, and the other for the bridge. Those heading for the blockhouse managed to approach as close as 30 meters to the French trenches but were stuck there. They tried to move ahead using the communication trench. However, because there were no support trenches and the squad was completely exposed to mitrailleuse fire, they found a corner and held there.[201]

One corporal and two combat engineers tried to approach the trenches, but one of the combat engineers was killed. The other was also shot when he tried to cut a wire. The group heading for the bridge was exposed to heavy fire from its right and stalled inside the river bed. Infantry fire from the Turkish side tried to support them, but they could not move any further.[202]

A soldier was dispatched from the Regiment to the group to understand why the troop could not move. The soldiers said:[203]

> *The enemy had a battalion in Zeytinlik. They ran away when they saw us. We cannot move any further because they are pouring fire from their mitrailleuse.*

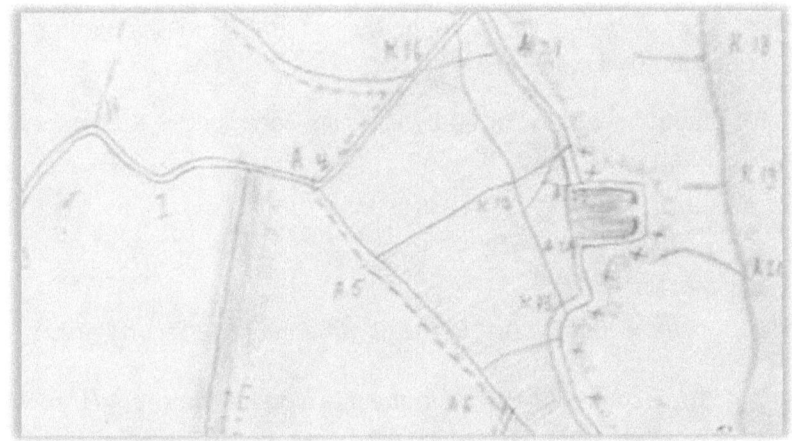

Figure 14: The protrusion of the French trenches into Yassıtepe according to a French map (K18, K19, K20, J' are the Turkish trenches across from the protrusion).

What these soldiers had seen was not a battalion, but the French patrol columns. Ahmet Nuri Bey sent two more squads to the area for support. Seeing the Turkish soldiers, the French patrol columns jumped back to their trenches and opened intense fire. The French artillery started shelling the upper slopes of the river in an attempt to block the support forces from coming. The Turkish detachment was having a difficult time. Ahmet Nuri Bey mobilized a gendarmerie platoon of 25 soldiers under the command of Lt. Halil Efendi, and added an engineer sergeant and two combat engineers to the platoon.[204]

When the support troops arrived, the detachment launched an attack.

It first detonated dynamites and destroyed part of the blockhouse. It threw bombs at the French soldiers inside the blockhouse and caused some losses but was unable to tear down the trench. Combat engineers damaged the wires surrounding the blockhouse. However, it also became impossible to hold against the relentless fire from all sides. The fiercest fire came from the right side of the river.

Furthermore, the French still had more forces inside the trenches. Taking these factors into account, Major Ahmet Nuri Bey ordered the Turkish forces to withdraw.[205]

This operation was reported by Division Commander Kâzım Bey to Fevzi Pasha as follows: [206]

> 13 August 331 [26 August 1915]   6:00 am
> Observation Post
>
> 'Morning Report' to the Command of the Second Area

1. The heavy artillery fire in the morning hit the enemy trenches at the Kerevizdere, causing some damage.

2. After the fire, three squads consisting of combat engineers and infantry were sent at 7:20 pm in two directions - one group heading to the bridge, and the other to the front of the trenches. They were subsequently reinforced with two more squads. These were exposed to the searchlight of the enemy and heavy infantry fire from the right along the Kerevizdere. To enable an attack, they were supported from the back by a troop of twenty-five volunteers led by an officer candidate. Under the artillery, grenade and machine gun fire of the enemy, they managed to approach the wires, and combat engineers managed to cut part of the wires and detonate the explosives. The infantry approached even further and started to throw their hand grenades under intense enemy fire. 12 men fell martyr and 15 were wounded when the enemy responded fiercely from all directions, and they were not able to enter the [enemy] trenches as these were already occupied by a company. The fallen soldiers and the wounded were subsequently brought back. Enemy skirmishers were detected along the Kerevizdere.

3. *In Section 8, where the enemy corpses are, the enemy is piling up sandbags and elevating the bomber's pit, and it seems they want to put some of our trenches under flanking fire. Our artillery will be shelling this position today.*

4. *No change in the situation. The soldiers were given the full ration. Enemy fire has been intense in Kerevizdere, and infantry fire and massive bombs have been deployed in other parts of our front.*

Commander of the
14th Division
Lt. Colonel [Kâzım]

Handover of the battalions of the 42nd Regiment

On 26 August, one day after the attack, the 1st Battalion was relieved in place by the 3rd Battalion. The 3rd Battalion became responsible for the area starting from the south side of Kansızdere, and the 2nd Battalion from the north. At 3:30 pm, the French artillery fire started, and the Turkish artillery responded shortly afterward. When the Turkish artillery damaged the front line, some black soldiers wearing turbans in the French trenches were seen running to the second line. A mountain gun was placed next to the existing machine gun to increase damage to the blockhouse.[207]

After 10 pm, the Metropolitan Brigade (175th Regiment and 1st African Regiment) relieved the French Colonial Brigade (54th and 56th Colonial Regiments) from the front line.[208]

Attacks on the French trenches

At 2:10 am on 27 August, two corporals from the 12th Company of the 42nd Regiment succeeded in entering the observation post that the French had extended towards the Turkish trenches. This caught the French by surprise. They destroyed some of the sandbags and carried some back to Turkish trenches, weakening the French front facing the Turkish lines. The Turks opened continuous fire.[209]

A squad from the 2nd Battalion and an engineering detachment were also sent to the French blockhouse. They approached the blockhouse, threw grenades, and detonated two sticks of dynamite. At 4:20 am, they came back without any casualties. Starting from 6 am until noon, the French pounded the Turkish trenches with mortar fire. They started again at 4:40 pm and continued for an hour.[210]

After 7 pm, they started pummelling the left side of Kerevizdere for half an hour, but only damaged a few sandbags. The Turkish mountain gun also started firing and two of its shells hit the French blockhouse, causing significant damage. Immediately afterwards, a Turkish squad launched an attack to the blockhouse, but could not make it to the other side due to intense machine gun fire. An engineering detachment, on the other hand, succeeded in approaching it as close as 15-20 steps away, and detonated their dynamite, damaging the blockhouse.[211]

A Turkish blockhouse against the French blockhouse

The French blockhouse was a serious threat for the Turks, but despite numerous raids to either seize it or render it dysfunctional, they had not succeeded. On 28 August, the 14th Division ordered the construction of a blockhouse on the Turkish side and the work started right away.[212]

At 9 am on the same day, the French opened mortar fire for around half an hour. Intermittent artillery and gunfire continued throughout the day, and at 4:40 pm the French started pounding the right flanks of the 42nd Regiment (i.e., north of Kansızdere). Turkish batteries responded immediately, triggering an artillery battle between the two sides that continued for about an hour. At 8 pm, a squad was sent out to destroy the French trenches. This squad approached until they were 15 steps away and threw their hand grenades. Light infantry fire continued throughout the night.[213]

The French were firing more than usual, and the Division warned the 42nd Regiment of a possible attack:[214]

To the Command of the 42nd Regiment

16 August 331 [29 August 1915]

Considering the aimless and senseless enemy artillery fire in recent days, it is likely that they have acquired new ammunition and will use this as an opportunity to attack. We must be alert to this possibility. God willing, and as before, such an attempt will no doubt be destroyed by our shining bayonets.

Commander of the
14th Division Lt.
Col. Kâzım

On the same day, the companies of the 1st Battalion relieved the 3rd Battalion, which subsequently left for Soğanlıdere. Under the defensive fire of patrol columns, the Turks continued to build their blockhouse.[215]

It remained calm until 3 pm the next day. Then the French started firing and some of the mortar and artillery shells landed in the Turkish front lines, causing major damage to the trenches of the 7th and 8th Battalions and to the dugouts. Many soldiers were wounded or died under the rubble. At 11 pm, the French started to pound the Turkish side with fierce grenade, mortar and gunfire in an attempt to prevent the construction of the blockhouse. The Turks fired back, and the clashes continued for about half an hour. A few French soldiers attempted to attack, but were pushed back. The Turks spent the whole night trying to rebuild the trenches, but some parts could not be repaired and remained open.[216].

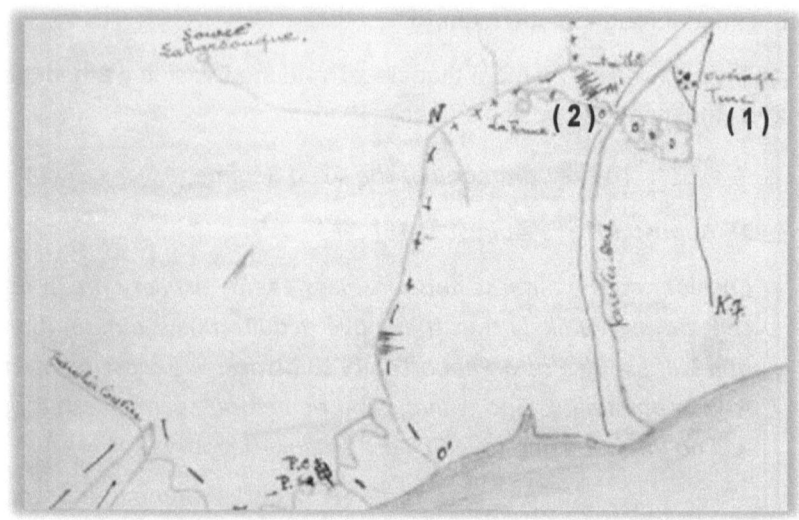

Figure 15: A section of French map showing the Turkish blockhouse; 1 - Turkish blockhouse, 2- French blockhouse Matillo (For the original map, see Document 4, p. 139).

In the meantime, Turkish artillery batteries continued to target the French front. The Turkish batteries on the Anatolian side - which had been silent for eight days - started to shoot as well. Artillery Major Aubry was killed by an artillery shell.[217]

Dr. Vassal, who witnessed the incident, wrote about it in a letter to his wife:[218]

> At about 8, a group of twenty to twenty-five persons could be seen from Achi Baba. The Turks directed on this spot a '150' shell, charged with a quantity of lead bullets. It burst a dozen yards overhead. Close to these casks, riddled like sieves, lay a

dozen soldiers bathed in blood.

I arrived ten minutes later. Four were dead—Artillery Major Aubry, another European, and two Senegalese. Two wounded had already been picked up. I turned my attention to the others, and sent to the dressing station for stretchers, vehicles, and doctors.

The major was killed almost by accident as he was just passing. He was caught full in the chest by shrapnel, and died instantly. Four more wounded won't live. You see that the Turks still have munitions — and better ones."

That same evening, Turkish artillery started pounding the French second line. Four soldiers from the French battalion died and 25 were wounded.[219]

The Turkish artillery was a constant problem for the French forces at Gallipoli[(I)]. The Allies tried to surmount this problem by opening naval fire towards the Turkish artillery. However, when German submarines started to cruise in the waters of the strait, it became increasingly difficult for the Allied navy to support its land forces. This enabled Turkish artillery batteries on the Asian side to become more

---

[I] When **General Gouraud** was the Commander of the French C.E.O., he had proposed a landing on the Anatolian side to stop the artillery attacks against the French rear lines. After he was wounded, **General Bailloud** replaced him and continued to insist that two of the three new British divisions execute a landing on the Asian shores. He even proposed that the French government insist upon this course of action. The French Minister of Defense **Millerand** wrote a letter to to his British counterpart Kitchener, but General Hamilton could not give up on his plans for the Suvla campaign due to a temporary difficulty caused by the Turkish artillery. Sir Ian Hamilton was convinced that the Turkish artillery on the Asian side would automatically stop firing if his main attack plan were to succeed (*Birinci Dünya Savaşı'nda Çanakkale Cephesi*, V.5, 3rd Book, p.271).

active. By the end of July, the French rear zones were under constant Turkish artillery fire, and this was taking its toll on the colonial soldiers.[220]

Over the last few days of August, the Turks also fired howitzer shells towards the French rear lines causing casualties, loss of animals, and physical damage.[221]

Letter from the Turkish commander to occupying soldiers

The trenches in Gallipoli - which were very close to each other - often changed hands. In one such instance, when the French seized a Turkish trench, they found an interesting note in English left for them:[i]

> *We hear from prisoners taken lately that your officers do their best to make you believe that we Turcs kill and massacre our prisoners.*
>
> *Not only the international law but also our Religion, as well as Humanity, teach us to treat prisoners and wounded men kindly and considerately.*
>
> *Be sure, British soldiers, that we Turcs will wellcome every single man of your's who comes to us, and will look upon him as a brother, and see that he shall return safely to his Home, Wife and Children.*
>
> *The Commander in Chief
of the Turkish Forces
Sad-ul-Bahr*

---

[i] For the original, see Document 12, p.147 (It appears that the original note in English was also translated into French. Both documents were found in the French military archives. - Author's note).

Reconnaissance patrol reproaches

On 31 August, a squad from the 1st Battalion, under the command of Sergeant Hüseyin, was sent to prevent the construction of the French blockhouse. They tried very hard and succeeded in approaching as close as 25 meters from the blockhouse. They saw that the French were working on the new road next to the blockhouse and did not have a reconnaissance patrol in the vicinity. When they spotted two French soldiers stick out their heads from their trenches, they immediately responded by throwing two bombs and a dynamite. This triggered a serious response from the French, who opened intense fire that lasted for a quarter of an hour. In a moment of slightly lighter fire, the squad seized the opportunity to throw all of its remaining grenades, while retreating 15 meters to the left in the direction of the sea. They continued to watch the French trenches from there and eventually retreated completely. On their way back, they came across an observation squad of the 41st Regiment, who asked them angrily: [222]

> *Why did you throw grenades? You make the enemy suspicious and we suffer the consequences.*
>
> *The members of the squad replied;*
>
> *We are doing the task we have been assigned to do, which is to rise up against the enemy.*

The trench that could not be dug

The French had received intelligence that suggested the Turks would start a general assault against all Allied lines on 1 September. General Bailloud ordered the implementation of defensive measures in all trenches. These included the reinforcement of the first line, checking the loopholes, digging defence saps, and placing barbed wire in zigzags in front of the first line. He also ordered barbed wire to be placed immediately in front of the 'Masnou' defence line. Mitrailleuse tripods were to be installed in different spots so that the machine guns could be moved around quickly.[223]

The Turks were making similar preparations. The Turkish trenches at Kerevizdere had a number of significant disadvantages with regards to their location, quality and quantity. The orders from 5th Corps were to improve the existing ones and dig new trenches where needed. The Turkish blockhouse that was built in response to the French 'Matillo' blockhouse at the mouth of the Kerevizdere was fortified, covered with iron, and topped with soil. The communication trench to the blockhouse was deepened.[224]

New trenches were dug behind the first line to form a potential line of defence. These were dug around Lahnadere, right across from the Kerevizdere, so that they could target the river valley. However, it was impossible to dig in some parts of the terrain. Ahmet Nuri Bey's report to the Division said:[225]

> *As the whole first aid station and its vicinity are a bed of fallen soldiers, it was not possible to dig any trenches.*

Curious enemy soldiers

Despite the relentless shower of bombs and shells, there were some interactions between the opposing sides that were quite extraordinary.

One such moment took place on the left flanks of the 42nd Regiment on 4 September 1915. The incident is described in the war diary of the 14th Division as follows:[226]

> *Yesterday, the enemy threw two papers written in German to the left flanks of the 42nd Regiment. In brief they claim that we*

> Turks who oppose them are actually Germans. They say they too are Germans. Therefore, there is no need to fight each other. Two enemy soldiers from the trenches opposite the 55th Regiment who could not suppress their curiosity then came out of their trenches and asked, 'Are you Germans or Turks?'. A soldier called Kurd Hasan knocked one of these soldiers to the ground. The other somehow escaped. They must have understood from this first-hand experience that we are indeed Turks.

Another incident that took place at Yassıtepe is described in the war diary of the 42nd Regiment:[227]

> From the enemy trenches across from A41/3 [41st Reg.3rd Bn.] they spoke in very clear Turkish – Come and surrender, there are nice clothes and food over here. The Germans have sacrificed you, brothers – and threw dry bread towards our trenches. They were given a response that befits Islam and Turkishness, though.

Another interesting incident was the call to prayer from the French trenches on 27 September. According to the war diary of the 55th Regiment:[228]

> At 9 pm on 13/14 September [27 September 1915], from the enemy trenches facing the 42nd Regiment, they recited with a very emotional voice, three Qul Huvvallahu Ahad followed by the Muslim call to prayer. I had my men reciprocate.

Six out of eight regiments of the French Oriental Expeditionary Corps were colonial regiments. Therefore, a considerable number of Muslim soldiers were fighting against the Turks.[229]

Dr. Vassal's account of an incident involving Muslim soldiers in the French Corps is quite striking:[230]

> I continued as far as the cemetery of our division. Some of our young soldiers were just finishing a burial. I stopped to talk to them. They were burying two blacks that were killed at the loopholes during the night. They finished their task while telling me a story.
>
> They cut two pieces of wood from a box of biscuits, joined them with a nail, and made crosses like all the others in the cemetery. The names of the Senegalese were carefully traced on the white wood.
>
> 'But perhaps these comrades are not Christian, and would prefer the crescent to the cross'.
>
> The little French peasants had not thought of that. The war has worked the miracle of making us all of the same religion!

From a cowardly soldier to the bravest...

The Balkan Wars, which had taken place shortly before the Gallipoli War, had resulted in a major defeat for the Turks. The army had disintegrated. All Ottoman lands on the European continent, aside from the area that stretched until the Meriç River, and the Aegean islands had been lost. This massive defeat had also led to a national awakening. Modernization efforts in the military had yielded results, with the army largely recovering in about a year. The commanding officers at Gallipoli were keen to undertake whatever was needed to avoid a similar disaster. A vivid example of this attitude can be found in Mustafa Kemal's orders for the 1 May 1915 offensive:[231]

> ... I cannot accept that there might be some, among us and the soldiers we command, who would rather not die than to let the Balkan shame repeat itself. If you feel there are some like that,

then we should be the ones to immediately execute them ourselves.

There was a similar understanding and sensitivity at the 42nd Regiment's front. The orders from the 14th Division were very clear: anyone who took a step back did not have a right to live in this country.[232]

In his memoirs, Ahmet Nuri Bey recounts an event he experienced as follows:[233]

At Çanakkale, some cowardly soldiers shot themselves in the hand or leg to escape from the battlefield. An order was issued to execute these soldiers. There were some cases like that in our regiment as well, but I never acquiesced to this order to execute these audacious men.

On one of those days, a soldier shot himself. The doctor issued a report, and the commanders of companies and battalions requested that he be executed to set a precedent. The enemy was attacking us at that moment, so I postponed the decision. Later, I told the soldier:

- It is better to fall a martyr by an enemy bullet rather than to die by a bullet from your brothers-in-arms, I said.

In the evening, I gave him two grenades and told him to throw them towards the enemy trenches that were 40-50 meters away, and once the enemy opened fire, to lie down among the thousands of soldiers who had died between the two trenches, and if he was not shot then, to say the codeword and come back. We repeated this three times and the soldier was never shot. On the contrary, a sergeant who was waiting for him in the trench fell a martyr.

I pardoned the soldier. The soldier's hand healed with some wound dressing. This soldier then volunteered to throw grenades at the enemy trenches during the night and showed much worthiness. When he laid down next to the dead bodies between the trenches, he searched the pockets of the dead and found seventy or eighty liras. I reported this soldier's situation to division commander Kâzım Karabekir, and he awarded him with a medal of war. I also promoted him to corporal. The faint-hearted soldier of the regiment became the bravest.

Intensive bombardment

Shells, bombs and mortar pouring over the trenches were part of an ordinary day in Gallipoli. According to the war diary of the 42nd Regiment, hundreds of shells, bombs and mortar bombs landed on their front every single day. Some days, however, the situation was even worse. 8 September 1915 was one such day.

At 8 pm on 8 September, two Allied torpedo boats moved towards Domuzdere. One started hitting the rear left trenches of the support line, and the other the right flanks of the second line. That same day, the French fired more than 1,400 artillery shells and mortars towards Zone 8.[234]

Most mortars were aimed at Kudsibey Hill. The French were trying to demolish the mine that Turks were building. This shooting caused serious damage to the area. 18 soldiers from the 55th Regiment lost their lives and 25 were wounded. One soldier went into shock.[235]

After the mortar fire stopped, the Turks spotted some soldiers with bayonets who were headed towards the first and second zones. The Turkish soldiers were ordered to prepare their bayonets, but the French did not dare to launch an attack. Some French soldiers put their casks on the bayonets and lifted them up. The Turks watched but did not make a move. [236]

At around the same time, the French also attacked the area defended by the 42nd Regiment, causing significant damage to the Turkish side with close to 1,500 shells and over 500 bombs. The 42nd Regiment lost 10 soldiers and 17 others were wounded. Another 12 soldiers were buried under the rubble, hurt but not severely wounded.

The French also directed their bombs towards the Turkish blockhouse at the mouth of the Kerevizdere, damaging part of the transportation road.[238]

The acting commander of the 10th Company Lt. Hakkı Efendi[(l)] was hit by a bomb and lost his life. The patrol that approached the French trenches returned from the no man's land with three rifles and five bayonets belonging to the Turks, along with two shovels and one pickaxe belonging to the French. They also informed the command that the French were busy digging.[239]

Picture 6: 1st Lt. İbrahim Hakkı[237]

The 42nd Regiment hands over the first line

On 10 September, Lt. Col. Kâzım ordered the 42nd Regiment to hand over the first line to the 41st Regiment. It had been close to a month and a half since the 42nd Regiment had taken charge of the first line,

---

[l] **İbrahim Hakkı:** Born in Istanbul, father's name: Emin, assigned to the 10th Division, 3rd Battalion of the 42nd Regiment. He fell at Kerevizdere. (Sayılır, *Tarihe Sığmayanlar,* p. 200).

42nd Regiment

and the hand-over to the next regiment would be carried out battalion by battalion. The new regiment would send its officers to the first line one day before the change-over, and receive all the necessary information regarding the trenches. After the change, Major Ahmet Nuri Bey, who had been the commander of the first line, would become the commander of the second line.[240]

At 11:20 pm on 10 September, the 1st Battalion of the 41st Regiment took over the position held by the 3rd Battalion of the 42nd Regiment, which began to head towards Soğanlıdere to rest. Fuad Bey, Commander of the 41st Regiment, also came to the first line.[241]

During the change-over, a French squad came out from the blockhouse to throw hand grenades at the Turkish blockhouse. However, they encountered fierce fire from the soldiers inside the blockhouse as well as the hillside, and were forced to run back.[242]

Light infantry fire continued until the morning. At 7 am, Lt. Col. Fuad Bey was shown around and given detailed information on the progress with the new trenches and the situation of the enemy. The whole area was subsequently handed over to his command, and the headquarters of the 42nd Regiment began its move to Soğanlıdere at noon.[243]

Lt. Col. Fuad Bey is shot

Soon after he took command of the first line, Lt. Col. Fuad Bey lost his life by a bullet to the head on 13 September. This happened while he was looking through the iron loophole at the bomber's pit, which the French had managed to advance a few days earlier[(I)]. Division

---

[I] One of the arms of the **Kerevizdere,** which was called **İsimsizdere** (literally 'Nameless River') throughout the war, is now called **Fuadbey Deresi (Fuadbey River).**

Commander Lt. Col. Kâzım Bey informed the troops of his death with the following words:[244]

Message to the Troops Regarding the Loss of Fuad Bey

The distinguished Commander of the 41st Regiment Lt. Col. Fuad Bey fell a martyr today at 10:20 am by an enemy infantry bullet, which hit him in the head while he was observing the enemy line from Şüheda Tepesi [Hill]. The loss of our distinguished colleague on duty is bound to exert a profound impact on all of us. However, rest assured that in defending our nation, he has attained the highest status and his name will never be forgotten. May God's blessings be upon all our martyrs. Commander of the 1st Battalion Major Nihad Bey has been appointed as the Commander of the 41st Regiment. I am certain that, with the grace of God, the valiant 41st Regiment will take revenge for the loss of its fallen commanders, officers and soldiers in the shortest time possible.

*Commander of the
14th Division
Lt. Col. Kâzım*

With Fuad Bey's death, Major Nihat Bey, the commander of the 1st Battalion, was appointed as the Regiment Commander.[245]

On 14 September, Ahmet Nuri Bey, who took over the second line from Osman Bey, first arranged the regiment's position. Together with the commander of the engineering battalion, he inspected the nighttime fortification work on the trenches. They determined all that needed to be done. The French bombardment of the second line later in the day damaged some of the communication lines.[246]

Nothing out of the ordinary happened in the following days. The Turks tried to repair the damaged trenches and communication lines.

42nd Regiment

A squad of the 42nd Regiment, positioned on the left flanks of the support line, detected a 10-man French reconnaissance patrol that tried to move in their direction. They opened fire and took one soldier prisoner. Two wounded soldiers from the French patrol rolled down to the river. The prisoner of war was identified as Moris Borpede of Marseilles and was sent to the 14th Division.[247]

Picture 7: Lt. Col. Fuad Bey [248]

When the day dawned, Turkish soldiers discovered that four other soldiers had not managed to run back to the French trenches - one was hiding in one of the wells to their left, and three other had lost their lives.[249]

Lt. Savl Hanik, Commander of the 12th Company who was in charge of the left flank, was informed of the situation. Orders were relayed over the phone to make sure the remaining soldier did not escape, and the guns and documents found on the dead soldiers were handed over to headquarters.

14 September and its aftermath

The Turks were working on a mine towards the French first line at Yassıtepe. The French had been listening to the Turks from the 12th to the 14th and were expecting two attacks – one on the first line, and the second at K22 (Kansızdere). The Turks, it appeared, were progressing fast with their mine and making preparations. In order to prevent these attacks, the engineering troops of the French 1st

Gallipoli 1915

Division started building a 'camouflet' (counter-mine)[I] with an entry point at K21. The French patrol observed the Turks reinforcing the

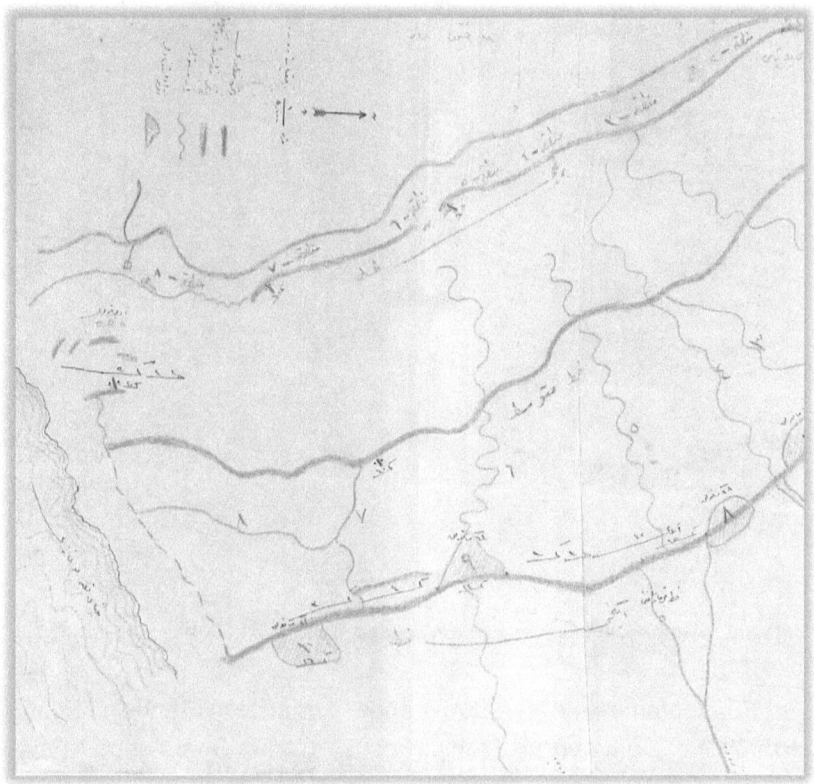

Figure 16: Turkish map showing first and second lines and communication trenches on 13 September 1915 (For the original map, see Document 9, p.144).

trenches and placing poles and barbed wire in front of their line. They opened fire on some Turkish trenches to deter them. They also observed the Turks repairing large segments of the second line.[250]

[I] **Camouflet (counter-mine):** See footnote on p.76-77

42nd Regiment

On 16 September, Turkish artillery units on the Asian side intensified their fire. Howitzers fired at the Seddulbahir area, killing one French soldier and wounding seven others near the seashore.[251]

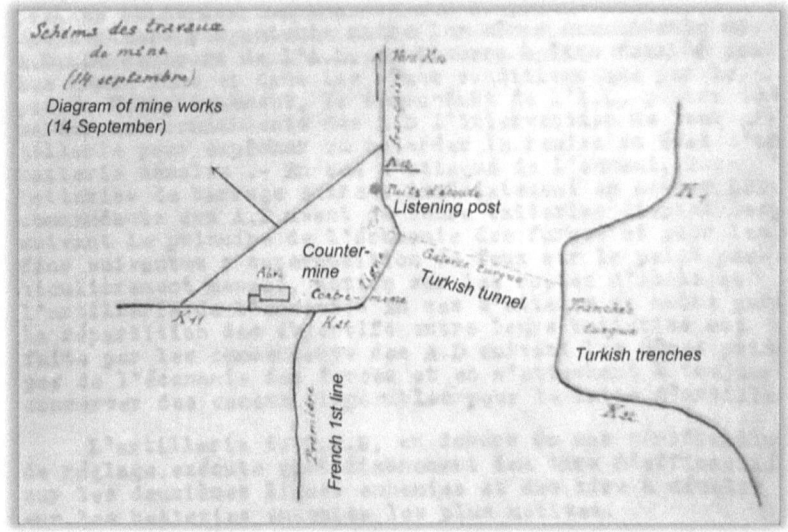

Figure 17: Turkish mine around Kansızdere as marked in a French diagram[252]

On 18 September, Army Commander Liman von Sanders, Southern Group Commander Vehip Pasha, Corps Commander Fevzi Pasha, and Division Commander Kâzım Bey came to inspect the second line.[253]

That same day, General Fourcade was appointed as commander of the 1st French Colonial Brigade. Lt. Col. Forey became the commander of the 175th Regiment while Lt. Col. Benoit took charge of the 176th Regiment.[254]

By 24 September, the French countermine had reached 5 meters in depth and 15 meters in length. Shells fired by the Turkish artillery at

Intepe struck the beach, killing 3 Senegalese soldiers and wounding 7 others. Heavy winds made it very difficult for the French to conduct troop landings from the ships.[255]

At 8 pm on 25 September, a French detachment launched an assault on the Turkish blockhouse. One French sergeant major and 6 soldiers lost their lives. Another detachment that launched a simultaneous attack lost its commanding sergeant.[256]

On 26 September, Turkish artillery on the Asian side pounded Seddulbahir and Morto Bay, killing 2 French officers and a number of Senegalese soldiers.

The French pull forces from the Gallipoli Front

For months now, the Allied Forces had not been able to secure the progress they had hoped for in Gallipoli. They were also aware that recent developments in the Balkans were not in their favour. They decided to move some of their forces from Gallipoli to the Salonica front.[257]

In a letter sent by the French War Ministry, General Bailloud was asked to form one division from two existing divisions of the C.E.O. and to send it to Salonica. The division was to consist of only European soldiers, and its commander would be General Bailloud.[258]

The reconstituted 2nd Division left Gallipoli at the end of September. Soon after that, General Brulard was appointed as Corps Commander of the C.E.O., and the name of the reorganized corps was changed to '*Corps Expeditionaire des Dardanelles*' (Expeditionary Corps of the Dardanelles). The new corps consisted of four colonial regiments and two heavy artillery units, as well as engineering and first aid units.[259] It also had an air force consisting of 14 planes.[260]

42nd Regiment

While the 2500-meter-long French trenches had been defended by two divisions up to this point, it was now the responsibility of only one.

42nd Regiment takes over the first line again

On 3 October, Commander of the 14th Division Kâzım Bey ordered Ahmet Nuri Bey to take over the first line:[261]

> To the Commander of the Second Line Major Nuri Bey
>
> As your regiment will be taking over all of the first line tomorrow, you must change with Tevfik Bey tonight and hand the command of the second line over to Major Aziz Bey.
>
> Commander of the
> Fourteenth Division
> Lt. Col. Kâzım

Ahmet Nuri Bey arrived at 4 pm to take over the first line from the commander of the 55th Regiment Major Tevfik Bey.[262] With this change-over, 42nd Regiment took charge of the right flank of the 14th Division and 41st Regiment took control of the left flank (see Fig. 18).

On the same day, the Turks finished the mine they had been digging toward the French line at Kansızdere. It was ready for detonation. As planned, gunfire from the trenches started at 5 pm and was accompanied by artillery fire. The French initially responded lightly, then with increasing gun, mitrailleuse and artillery fire, but failed to cause serious damage. At 5:30 pm, the mine was detonated as Turkish soldiers, who had fixed their bayonets, shouted 'Allah Allah'.[263]

The explosion happened five meters away from the French first line and caused only partial damage to the trenches, wounding a few

French soldiers. Turkish artillery fire, on the other hand, killed four soldiers and wounded eight others.[264]

Bilateral fire stopped for some time around 5:40 pm but continued lightly during the evening. The French shelled the support line intermittently and targeted the first aid station with big bombs.

On the other hand, the Turkish artillery, which started firing at 9 am on 4 October, caused serious damage. The French retaliated by pounding the trenches of the 42nd Regiment with 550 shells, 240 shrapnel shells, 45 heavy shells, and around 60 hand grenades.[265]

At 9:40 am on 5 October, the Turkish artillery on the Asian side pounded the shoreline where the French were positioned. At 9:45 am, a Turkish plane carried out a reconnaissance flight over the French trenches. Exchange of infantry fire and hand grenades continued during the whole day. To prevent the Turks from working on the blockhouse, the French deployed their machine gun at Yassıtepe throughout the evening.[266]

In the evening, the Turks also opened harassing fire when they realized the French were repairing their trenches. Although the French had thrown close to 600 shells of various kinds over the span of 24 hours, they failed to cause major damage.[267]

On 6 October, Turkish artillery was very effective and caused serious damage to the French front. The French responded by pounding the Turkish lines with around 500 shells, while the Turks continued building dugouts and fortifying their support trench.[268]

On 7 October, German engineering officer Lt. König was ordered to construct a countermine across the sap that the French were building at Cesetlertepe. Soldiers under the command of Lt. Mehmet Efendi started digging that same day. A reconnaissance patrol was sent out to prevent the French from working on their sap. They threw grenades at the trenches that the French had fortified.[269] Another patrol managed to bring back one rifle, two bags full of ammunition, and an unexploded bomb.[270]

On 9 October, the French pounded the Turkish trenches with shells and grenades. It was rainy and dark, and the Turks worried that the French would take advantage of the weather to launch an attack. They tried to counter this possibility with heavy gun and artillery fire, while French planes flew over the area on reconnaissance missions. On the Turkish side, everyone was busy digging trenches and mines.[271]

The French, on the other hand, focused on fortifying the Masnou trenches and building machine gun pits, bunkers and parapets. The Turks threw 30 hand grenades towards the Matillo blockhouse.[272]

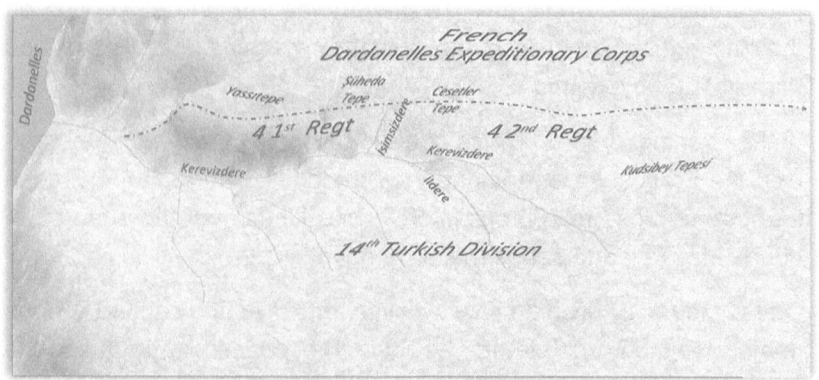

Figure 18: Position of the 42nd Regiment

On 10 October, Turkish detachments approached the French trenches, opened barrage fire and attacked the Matillo blockhouse with hand grenades. Turkish revolver cannons also targeted Matillo, while the soldiers in the trenches worked hard to complete the mines in Kansızdere.[273]

Barrage fire continued along the trenches on 12 October. The Turks continued to extend their mine toward the French trenches, while the French focused on extending their sap toward the Turkish trenches that they referred to as K5. They also started digging in the area around the listening post.[274]

On 15 October, Turkish detachments raided the French blockhouse. In the war diary of the French C.E.O., the incident is described as follows:[275]

> *At 3 am on 15 October, a group of Turks from the White trench threw hand grenades in front of Matillo. Sergeant Major Bernard and four of our bombers retaliated. They had just managed to push them back when an explosion occurred, and the central part of Matillo collapsed. 1 sergeant and 5 soldiers were buried under the rubble. Right after that, the Turks doubled their hand grenade and barrage fire, and their artillery began to pour shells towards the back of our parapets. The bombers of the Kerevizdere troop, Sergeant Bernard and his four men, jumped on the Turks who had hand grenades.*
>
> *Shortly thereafter, the 65th Artillery Unit arrived with half of its force and fired on the Turkish trenches and communication tunnels. Gilquin's company started shelling the white trenches and the lines behind it, while support forces of Senegalese soldiers made their way to Matillo with the commander of the battalion and Lt. Roques.*
>
> *The hand grenade battle continued as we tried to remove the rubble to save our men. Everyone who saw or heard that Sergeant Major Bernard and his four soldiers, who we thought were either dead or captured, were fighting the Turks in grey trenches*

> with hand grenades, was happy (we sent them hand grenades right away). Clashes continued even after dawn until 6 am - (Sergeant Major Bernard was wounded by a Turkish hand grenade) - we were then replaced by the next battalion on duty.

On 19 October, the French started an attack at 7:30 am with artillery fire and hand grenades. Most shots landed behind the Turkish regiment and did not cause damage. Gunfire was relatively lighter that day, and the French soldiers spent the whole day placing wires along the first and second lines at Cesetlertepe Hill.[276]

Bilateral artillery fire continued from the 20th to the 22nd of October. The Turkish soldiers continued to build trenches and dugouts, while the French shelled the second line and the left flank of the 42nd Regiment. A Turkish third lieutenant and soldier lost their lives.[277]

On 24 October, the French fired their mitrailleuse continuously. In 24 hours, they threw 419 bombs, 5 mortar shells, 100 shrapnel shells and numerous hand grenades at the Turkish trenches. Turkish artillery responded and, according to the soldiers in the observation post, was quite effective. The French forces facing the 42nd Regiment incurred serious damage. The Turks sent out reconnaissance patrols in the evening and opened fire on the French patrol units. Two French soldiers were killed, and the remaining soldiers ran back to their trenches.[278]

On 25 October, French shelling was even more intensive. In total, the French launched 720 artillery shells, 52 mortar shells, 24 shrapnel shells, and countless hand grenades. One of the mortar shells hit a dugout and two others hit the gunpowder and ammunition storage area, killing four soldiers and wounding eleven others. The 42nd Regiment wrote to ask the 14th Division to direct artillery fire at the French bombers:[279]

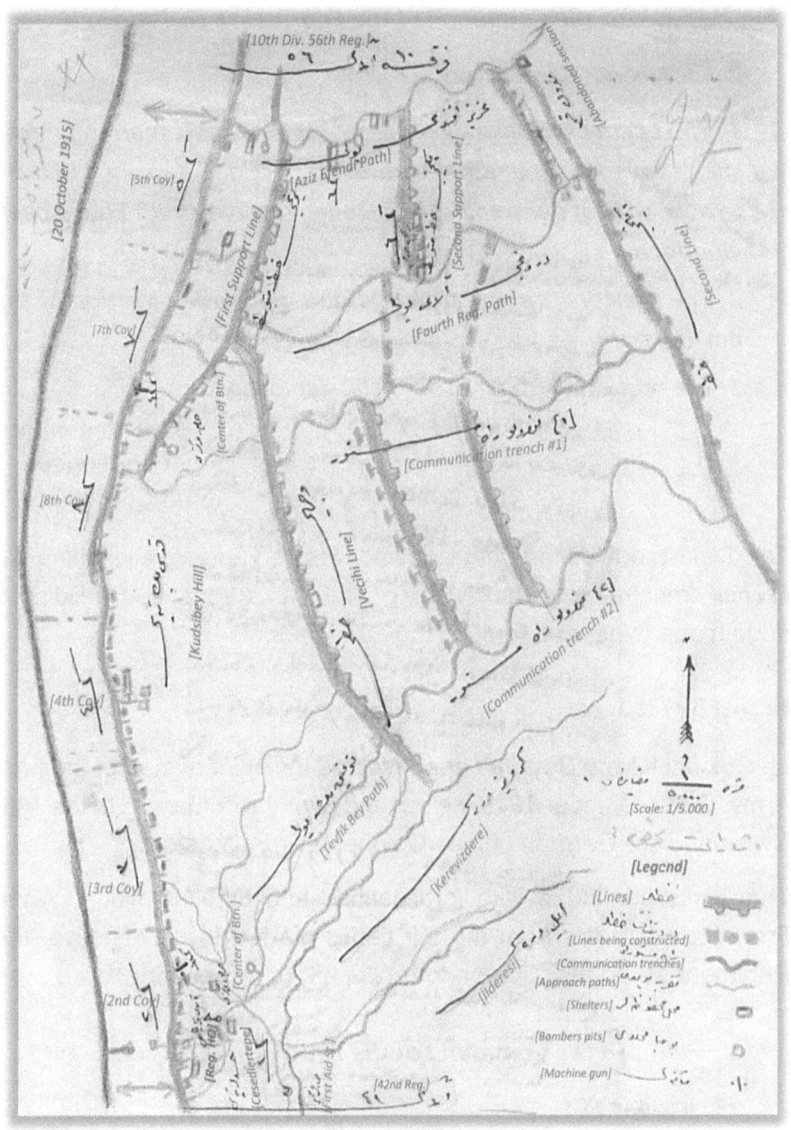

Figure 19: Turkish map showing the position of the 42th Regiment on 20 October 1915 [280]

42ⁿᵈ Regiment

> To the Command of the Fourteenth Division
>
> 24 October 1915 9:30 am
>
> 1- The enemy continues its mortar fire since this morning. Most shells have hit around the command post and Kudsibey Hill. Up to now, four of our soldiers have fallen martyrs and 11 have been wounded.
>
> 2- The mortars are probably situated along the direction of the narrow path.
>
> 3- We request that the artillery be deployed.
>
> 42nd Regiment
Commander
Major Ahmed Nuri

The Turkish artillery fire that followed was very effective in hitting the French trenches and their vicinity. The Turks continued building a dugout and mine, and fortified their trenches.

Kâzım Bey leaves

Lt. Colonel Kâzım Bey was appointed as the chief of staff of the First Army. On 24 October 1915, he handed over the command of the 14th Division to the German officer, Colonel Von Sodenstern.[281]

The Turks continued with fortifications and digging mines. When French artillery fire from the left flanks started to be effective, the Regiment asked the Division to retaliate with artillery fire:[282]

> To the Command of the Fourteenth Division,
>
> 28 October 1915
>
> The enemy has placed three shrapnel bomb cannons on the protruding zone at the right flank of the third zone. They have been

firing at our command post for half an hour. We request artillery fire to be opened on this position.

*42nd Regiment
Commander
Major Ahmed Nuri*

Mine wars intensify

A countermine built by Turkish engineering troops at Yassıtepe was detonated at 10:50 pm on 1 November. The blast destroyed the parapets along a 10-meter trench line and killed 2 French soldiers who were working underground. The Turks carried on with intensive artillery fire, while the French focused on digging a countermine.[283]

There was no major infantry activity on 3 November. The French were preparing to detonate their countermine at Yassıtepe, but Turkish engineering troops managed to detonate their mine first. The blast created a 9-meter wide crater. It demolished 15 meters of the French trenches and tore down a small blockhouse that they had built on an old mine crater.[284]

On 5 and 7 November, the French detonated two countermines. On 8 November, a mine detonated by the Turks created a 3-meter wide crater and destroyed 10 meters of the French trenches. That same day at 9:30 pm, the French blew up a countermine at Kansızdere (K21), and Turkish artillery on the Asian coast pounded the shores of Seddulbahir.[285]

On 11 November, French trenches along the coast, near the mouth of the Kerevizdere, were flooded with water.[286]

In the days that followed, both sides focused all their efforts on mine warfare. According to French records, the French miners even dug right into a Turkish mine. The two sides clashed inside the tunnels and one of the two Turkish miners lost his life.[287]

42ⁿᵈ Regiment

According to the records of the 14th Division, mines on both sides often came very close to each other, and miners were therefore ordered to always carry guns with them:[288]

> *The command of the first line's engineering detachment has informed us that in Zone Six[I], the enemy is digging a mine opposite ours but more towards the right. As a precaution, the soldiers are to carry knives and revolvers at all times.*

[I] The area around Şüheda Tepe (Hill).

Part 4

The Road to Victory

42nd Regiment Hands Over its Trenches

The following days passed with mutual shelling and mine warfare. Both sides increasingly chose to remain in their trenches. An order dated 12 November 1915 instructed the 14th Division to hand over its area of responsibility to the 20th Division. It asked that all necessary information be relayed to the advance guard of the incoming division. The advance guard, which arrived a day earlier than the rest of the Division, consisted of officers, non-commissioned officers, and a number of soldiers. Ahmet Nuri Bey gave the commanders and officers information regarding the terrain, the French forces, and the general situation of the regiment. He also explained how they protected their area during the day and night, how they defended themselves against heavy grenade and mortar fire, how to raid the enemy trenches, how to fortify the trenches, what needed to be done next, the layout of the communication trenches and the middle trenches, as well as the location of mortar emplacements. After the briefing, the battalion commanders went back to their division. One officer and ten soldiers from each incoming company stayed behind and were sent to the relevant companies in the trenches.[289]

The Turks continued with rifle fire to prevent the French from digging mines during the day and fortifying their trenches at night. During the evening, a reconnaissance patrol reported loud noises coming from the French squads, by which they understood that the French were still digging new mines. The Turks continued working on their mines as well. The French launched 368 shells, 7 mortar shells and 152 shrapnel shells in 24 hours.[290]

Freezing cold weather

Meanwhile the weather was becoming harsher and it was starting to feel like winter. On 17 November, the rainfall flooded the trenches. This prevented the 42nd Regiment from making the necessary fortifications, and they spent the next day trying to drain the trenches.[291]

The cold was a major problem for the French soldiers from the colonies. Already in August, Dr. Vassal had voiced his concerns about these soldiers:[292]

> *The Gallipoli sky, which was always a limpid blue unspotted by the smallest cloud, has been quite changed the last ten days. It is going to rain; it will turn cold. We are thinking of winter, and have begun to prepare winter quarters.*

What will our trenches be like? What will become of us? Some say that the Senegalese cannot stand the French winter, and that the Gallipoli winter is still more severe.

One of the main events in November occurred with the cold that came on 26 November. The severe rainfall that evening caused floods all over Gallipoli and was especially harsh around Suvla. The main trenches, dugouts and communication trenches flooded, and both sides lost many men who either drowned or were washed away. Both sides were trying hard to survive the same disaster and stopped firing at each other. It was as if a truce had naturally emerged out of the graveness of the situation. The next day brought very cold north-eastern winds, which turned into a heavy snow storm in the evening. Temperatures went down to -10°C. It continued throughout the 28th and 29th of November, and many soldiers on both sides froze to death. Hundreds were hospitalized and had to be sent back.[293]

The situation in Seddulbahir was slightly better, but Senegalese soldiers were suffering greatly, with many starting to get frostbite on their hands and feet. The French recorded temperatures of -8°C in their trenches. Due to the freezing cold and numerous soldiers with pulmonary problems, the French were forced to pull back 467 Senegalese and Creole soldiers from the front line. The remaining colonial soldiers were in no position to hold weapons or resist a Turkish attack either, because their hands had turned numb from the cold. These soldiers could not even help with trench fortifications anymore. The French had only their European soldiers to rely on, but these were few, and they were the last reserve available. The French asked their headquarters for an urgent reinforcement of European soldiers to replace the Senegalese and Creole soldiers in the trenches.[294]

Turkish Victory

After the changeover between the 14th and 20th Divisions, the 42nd Regiment left for Soğanlıdere and stayed there until the end of December. On 3 January 1916, it was sent to Kumtepe on the western coast of the Gallipoli peninsula.

Meanwhile, the Allied Forces had accepted their defeat and started retreating in December, and the last of the Allied troops had left Gallipoli by 9 January 1916. The Turks had won. The new commander of the 14th Division sent a letter to the 42nd Regiment commending them for this success:

> *To the Command of the 42nd Regiment*
>
> *Congratulations are in order for the Command of the Southern Group regarding the general victory. Our officers and soldiers have fought hand to hand for months and have shown great resilience that has shaken the enemy, and their sacrifices are at the heart of this victory. May God let their actions lead to similar victories everywhere.*
>
> *Commander of the*
Fourteenth Division
Colonel Von Sodenstern

In his memoirs, Ahmet Nuri Bey recounts walking around in the trenches that the French had evacuated: [295]

> *After the enemy ran away, I walked around the enemy trenches across from us. On a road, the French had written:*
>
> *" L'honeur au Turc (The honour belongs to the Turks) "*

Nuri Bey Fountain

In honour of all the fallen officers and soldiers of the 42nd Regiment,

Ahmet Nuri Bey commissioned a fountain in Kerevizdere (see Picture 8). He discusses the fountain in his memoirs as follows:[296]

> With the help of the non-Muslim artisan soldiers, I had a nice cut stone fountain built at Soğanlıdere. I had the following epitaph written on it:
>
> "Al-Fatiha to the souls of the fallen commanders, officers and soldiers of the 42nd Regiment". It says on it, "Nuri Bey Fountain".

The 42nd Regiment leaves Gallipoli

After the Allies withdrew their forces from Gallipoli, the 42nd Regiment left its position to the 12th Division and departed from Kumtepe on 10 January 1916. Together with the rest of the 14th Division, it left the Gallipoli peninsula on 11 January. In his memoirs, Ahmet Nuri Bey recounts how the war-torn and exhausted troops who made their way to their new location were further challenged by the newly appointed Division Commander:

> The day after the enemy fled Çanakkale, we received orders to depart by land to Istanbul. Kâzım Karabekir had been appointed as corps commander to the Mosul front. He was replaced by a German called Von Dozestern [von Sodenstern]. He was an enemy to the Turks. He ordered military training all the way from Çanakkale to Çekmece. Half of the Division got sick and could not continue. Some died. The enemy had left in January, so it was winter. We complained to the commanders. When the division arrived in Büyükçekmece, the German was taken away from the division. I became the acting commander. They invited me to the general headquarters and asked me about Von Dozestern's [sic] mistakes;

Picture 8: Nuri Bey Fountain[1]
Epitaph:
Commander of the 42nd Regiment Nuri Bey Fountain.
Al-Fatiha to the souls of the officers and soldiers who fell martyr at the hills of Kerevizdere. Çanakkale 1331 1333 [1915] "

[1] The photograph is from the author's family album.

- My superiors know better. I cannot criticize a superior, I said.

- If you were the division commander, what would you have done? they said.

- Since there was no enemy around us, I would have thought of securing food and accommodation for the regiment and the battalion, and I would have moved them separately, I said.

The Germans were very angry with my answer because they wanted to prove Van Dozestern [sic] right. The Division was sent from Çekmeceler to Üsküdar, Bağlarbaşı. Ali Fuad Pasha[I] *was appointed as Division Commander.* [297]

The 42nd Regiment after the Dardanelles Campaign

Although the Turkish Army ultimately achieved a major victory and forced the Allied forces out of Gallipoli, wars along other fronts were not over for the Ottoman Empire. Conflicts continued in the Caucasus, Iraq, Palestine and Hejaz fronts. Troops from Gallipoli were quickly redeployed in other fronts. The next destination for the 42nd Regiment was also determined: it was to be the Hejaz Front.

In early 1916, Cemal Pasha was busy planning an operation to the Suez Canal. The Ottomans expected help from Sharif Hussein, the Emir of Mecca, and were giving him financial support. While Sharif Hussein appeared to be close to the Ottomans, he was also taking arms and money from the British and the French, and was preparing for revolt. He found an opportunity when the British evacuated Gallipoli and started moving their forces to Egypt. On 23 May 1916, he

---

[I] **Ali Fuad Cebesoy**

42nd Regiment

revolted against the Ottomans and besieged Medina on 5 June. Fahreddin Pasha was appointed as the Commander of the Hejaz Expeditionary Force (Hicaz Kuvve-i Seferiyesi Komutanlığı).[298]

The 42nd Regiment was reorganized with minor additions of force, became the "Nuri Bey Müfrezesi" ('Nuri Bey Detachment'), and was sent to Medina. It made its way through the siege on 8 June 1916 and joined the Hejaz Expeditionary Force in Medina.[II] For two years, the 42nd Regiment fought in numerous battles - not only against its opponents, but also against the difficult conditions of the desert, including thirst, hunger and disease. It defended Medina from the

Picture 9: Fahreddin Pasha decorating the Regiment Standard with the medal.[I]

[I] The photograph is from the author's family album.

[II] "The forces sent to Medina from the North is the 42nd Regiment, known for its gallantry in Gallipoli, and it arrived in Medina on 8-9 June" (Kıcıman, *Medine Müdafaası*, p.37).

Arabs and British, and lost a significant part of its force. For its gallantry in the Hejaz, the regiment was decorated with silver Imtiyaz medals.

Having lost nearly all its men in the Hejaz, the 42nd Regiment was reconstituted in 1921, and this time fought against the Greek Army at Sakarya. Once again, almost all its soldiers, including then-commander Hüseyin Avni Bey, lost their lives in battle. Nevertheless, the Regiment played a pivotal role in stopping the advance of Greek forces towards Ankara.[299]

Epilogue...

This book tells the true story of the 42nd Regiment in Gallipoli. The story of the 42nd Regiment is only one of many stories of the soldiers and troops whose sacrifice and bravery made the establishment of the Republic of Turkey possible.

Documents

42nd Regiment

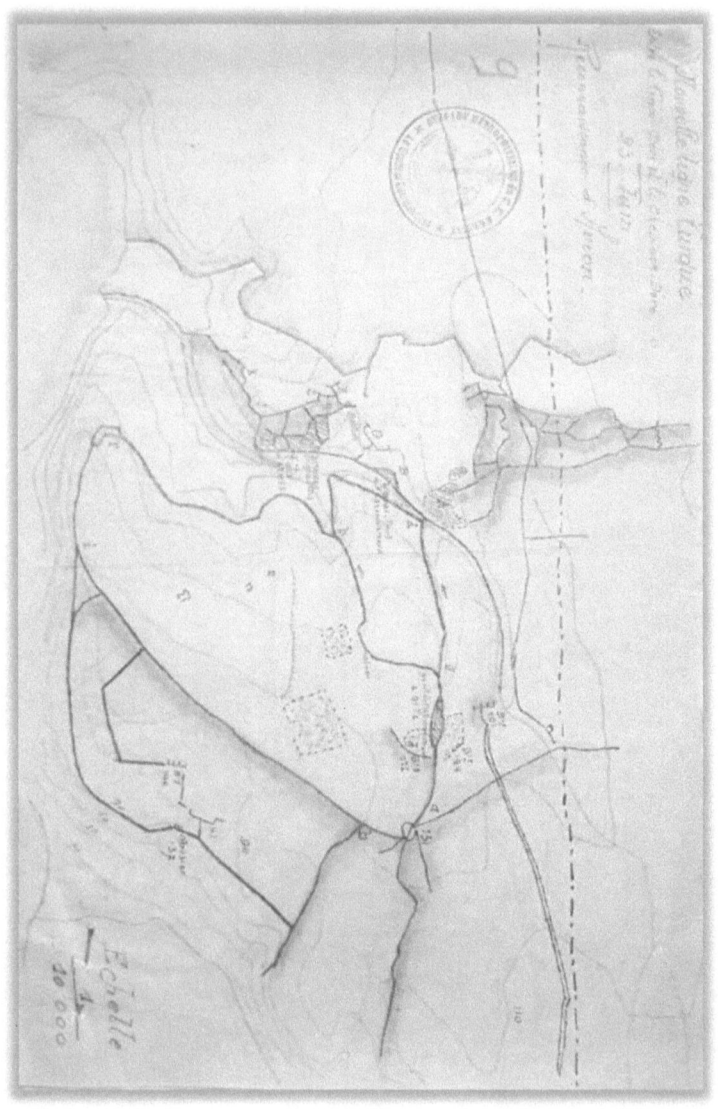

Document 1: French map showing the new Turkish line on 23 July 1915.[300]

Gallipoli 1915

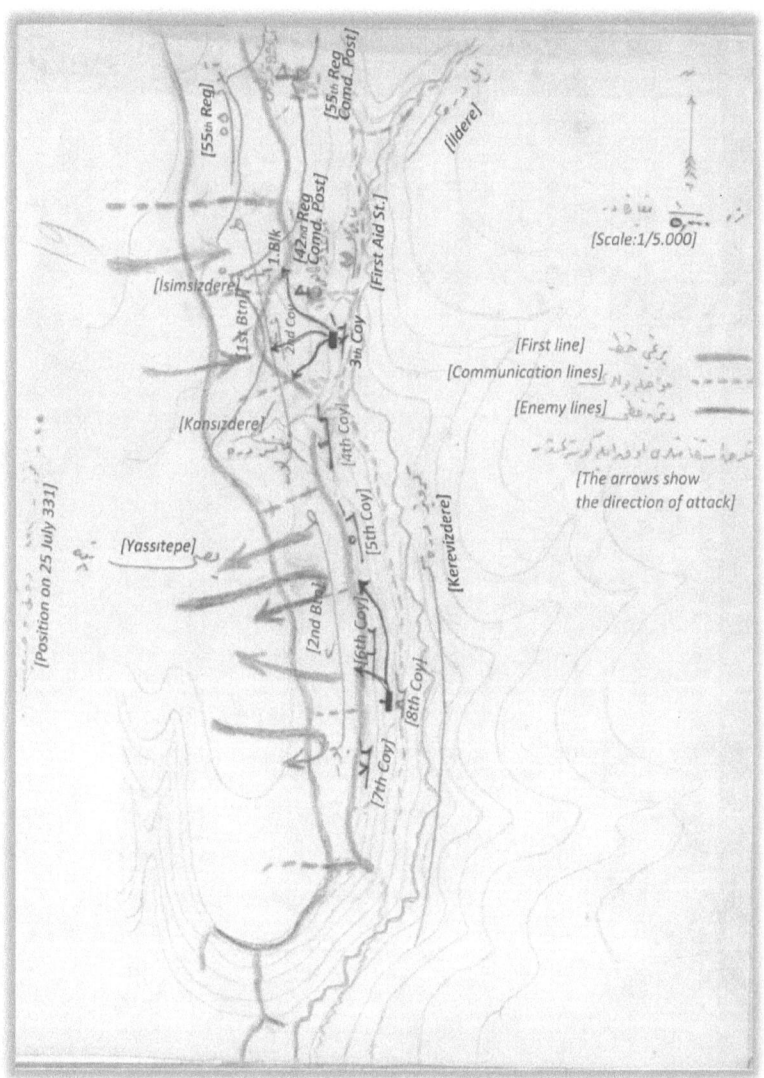

Document 2: Turkish map showing the French attack and Turkish counter-attack on 7 August 1915 at Kerevizdere. [301]

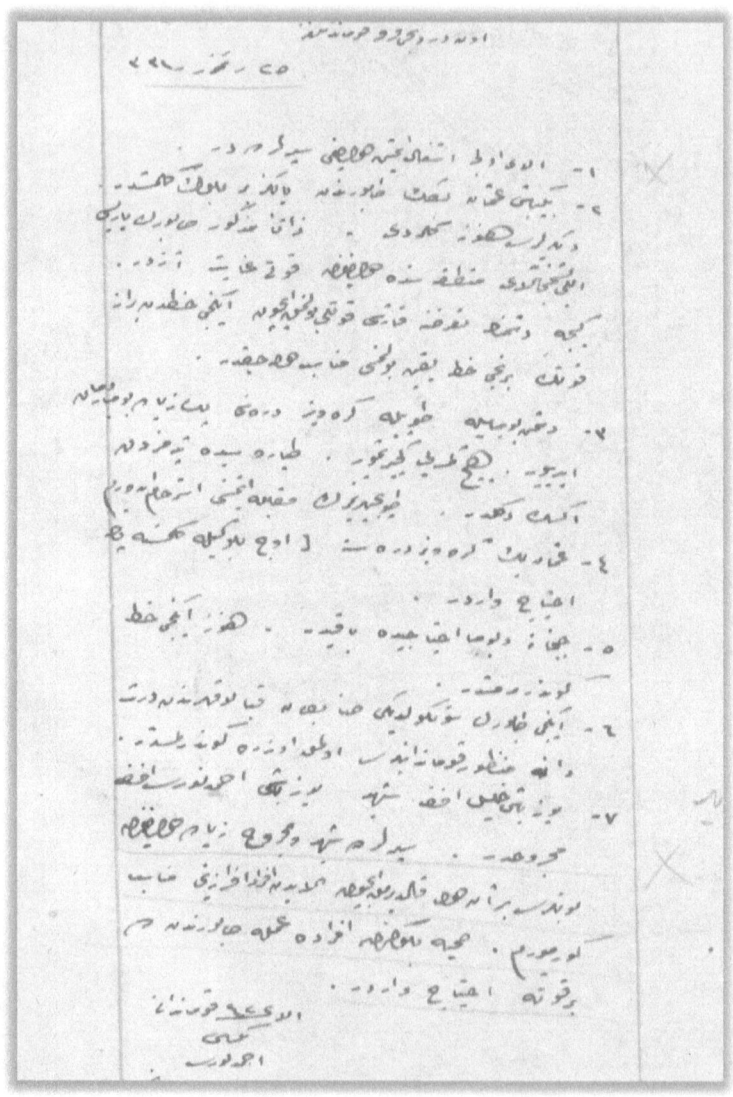

***Document 3:** The war report of Major Ahmet Nuri Bey on the clashes of 7 August 1915 sent to 14th Division.*[302]

Gallipoli 1915

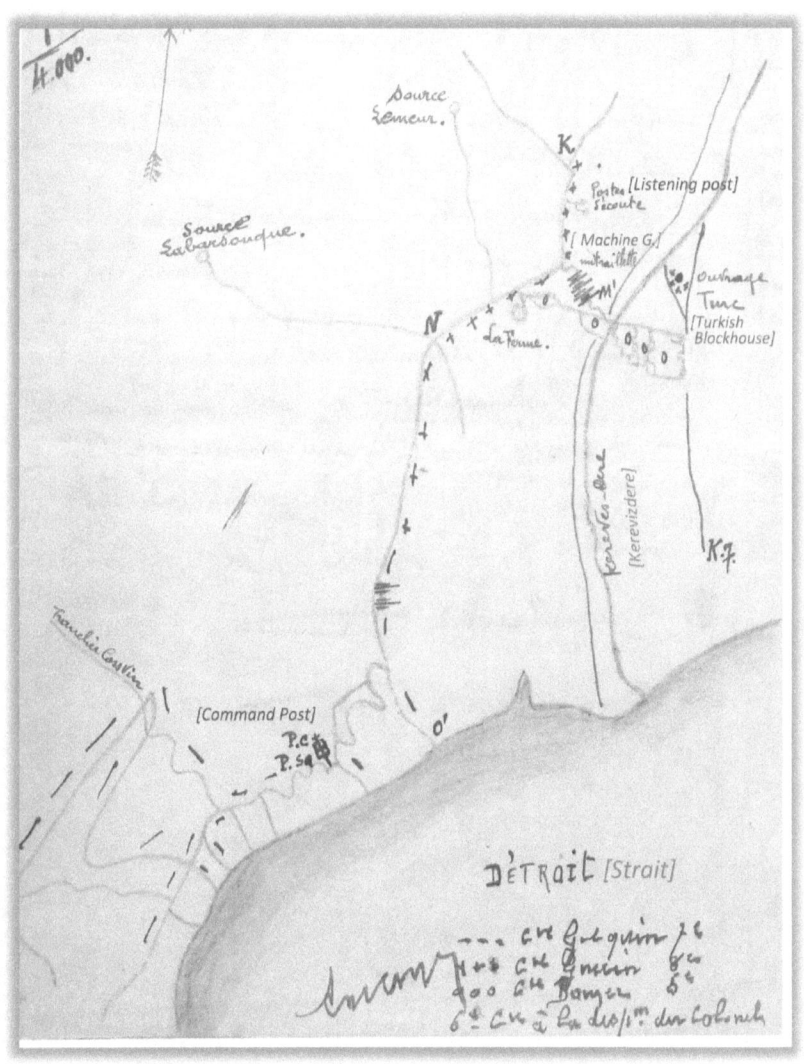

Document 4: French map showing the Turkish blockhouse.[303]

42nd Regiment

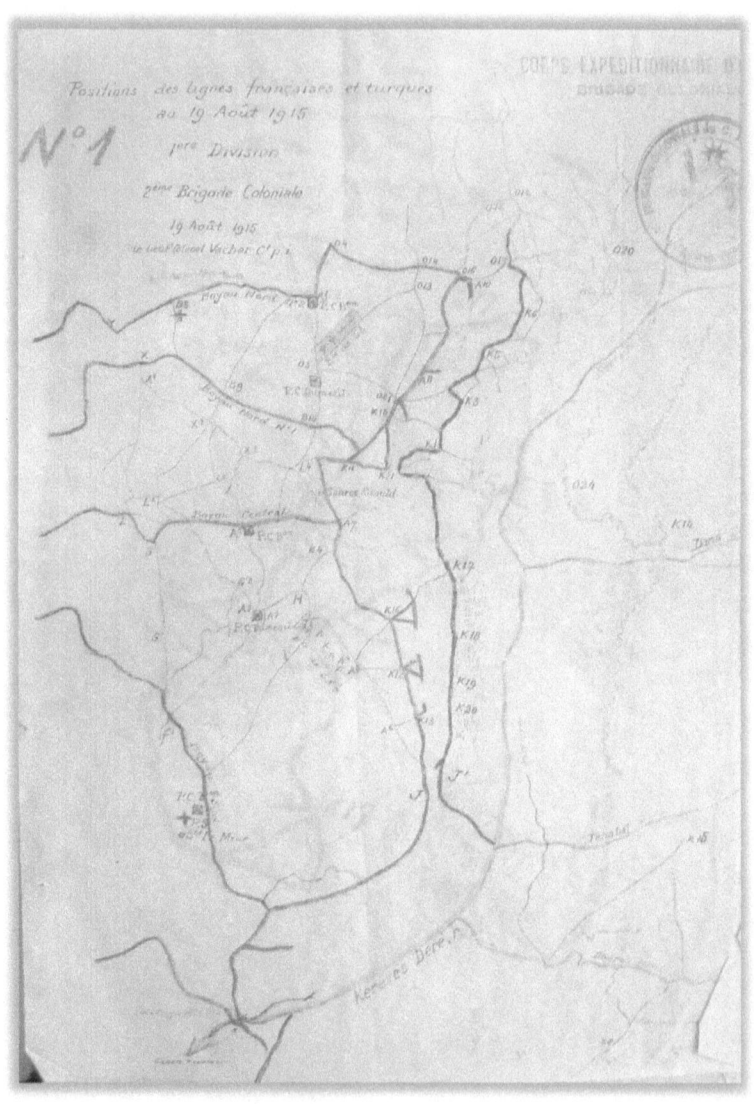

Document 5: French map showing the French and Turkish lines on 19 August 1915 at Kerevizdere. [304]

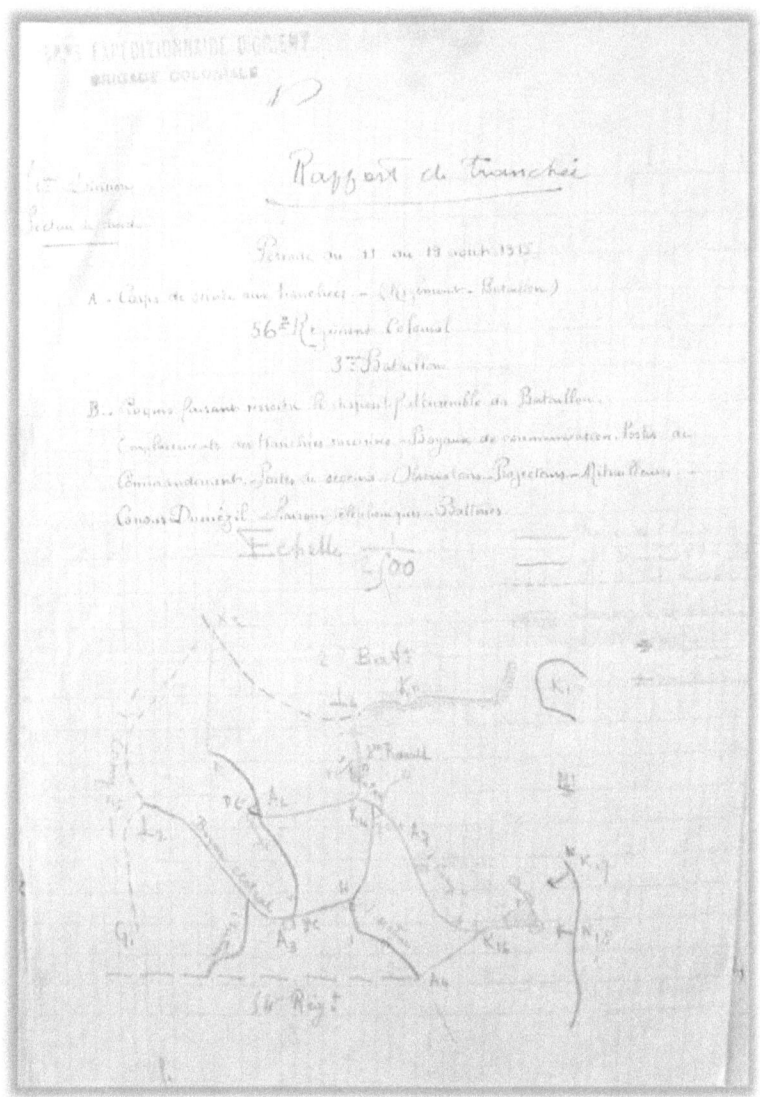

Document 6: 56th Colonial Regiment's trench report.[305]

42nd Regiment

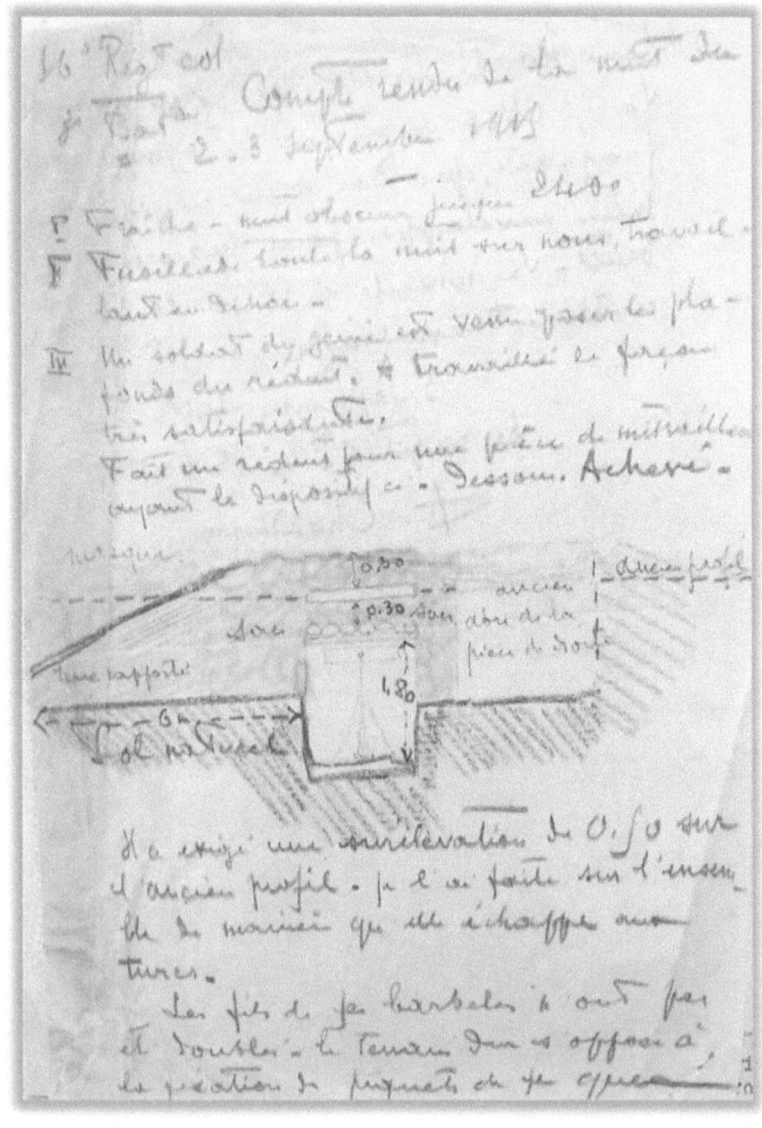

Document 7: The situation report of the 56th Colonial Regiment for the night of 2 September 1915.[306]

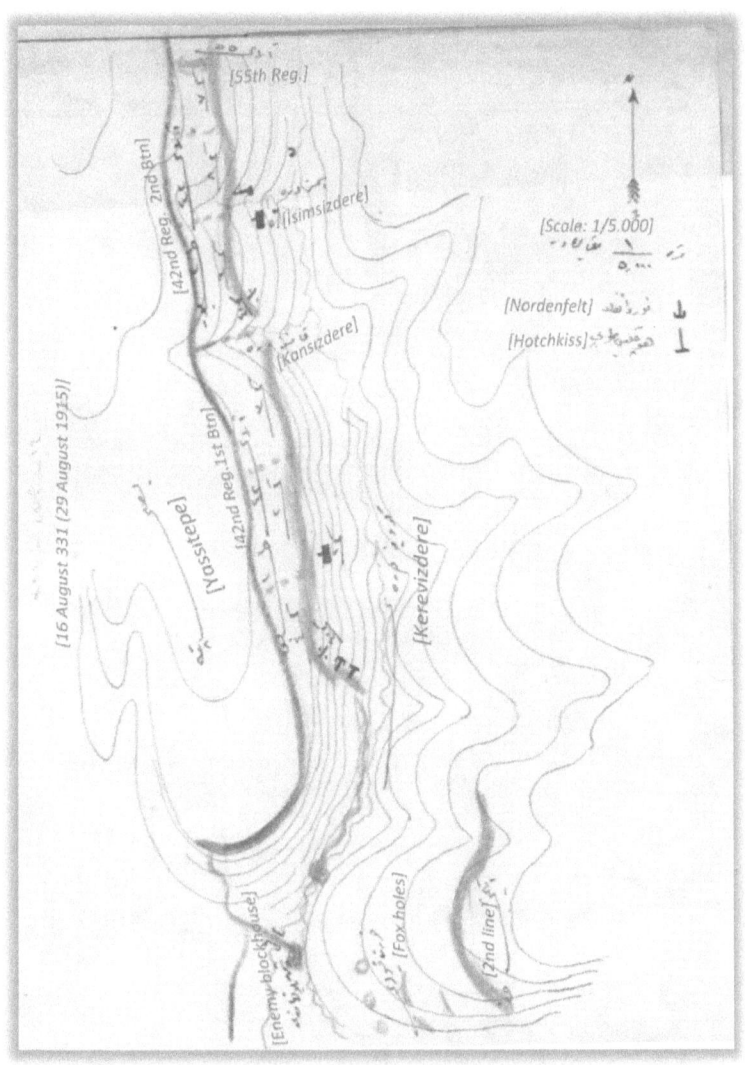

Document 8: Turkish map showing the position of the 42nd Regiment at Kerevizdere on 29 August 1915. [307]

42nd Regiment

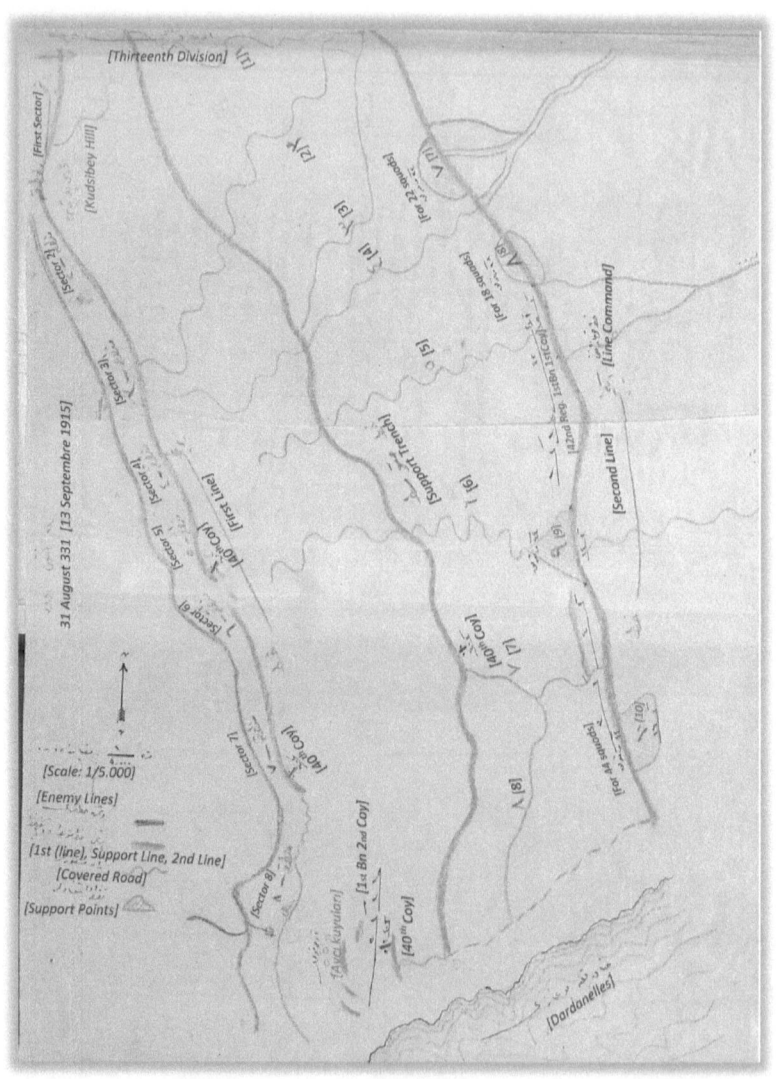

Document 9: Turkish map showing the Turkish trenches and communication lines. [308]

Gallipoli 1915

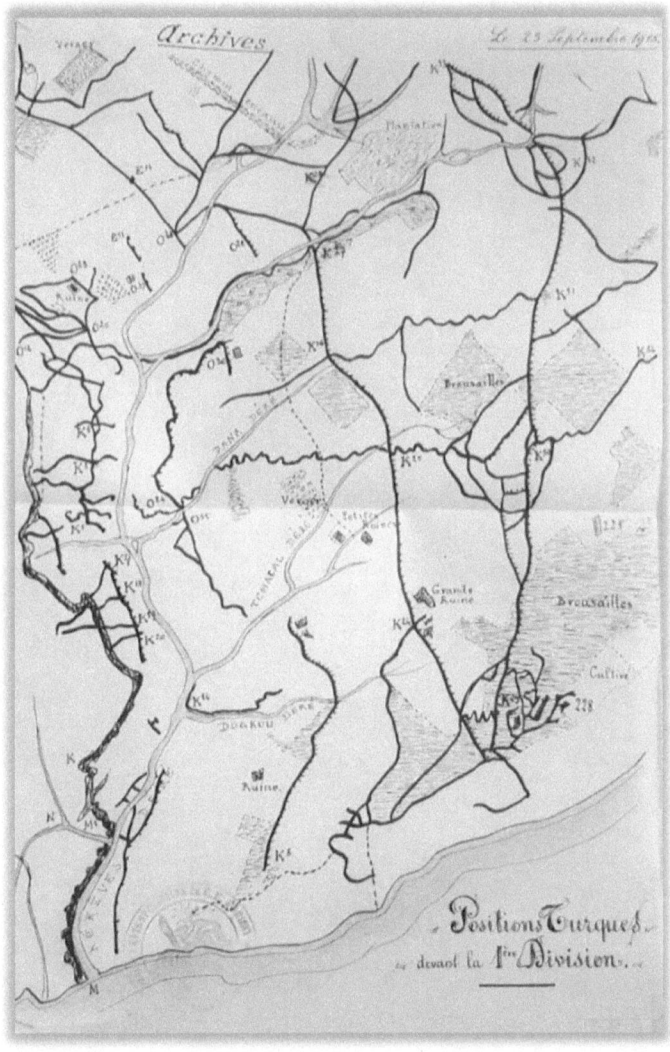

Document 10: French map showing the position of the Turks opposite the French 1st Division. [309]

42nd Regiment

Document 11: French operation report showing the list of French casualties in the 7 August attack.[310]

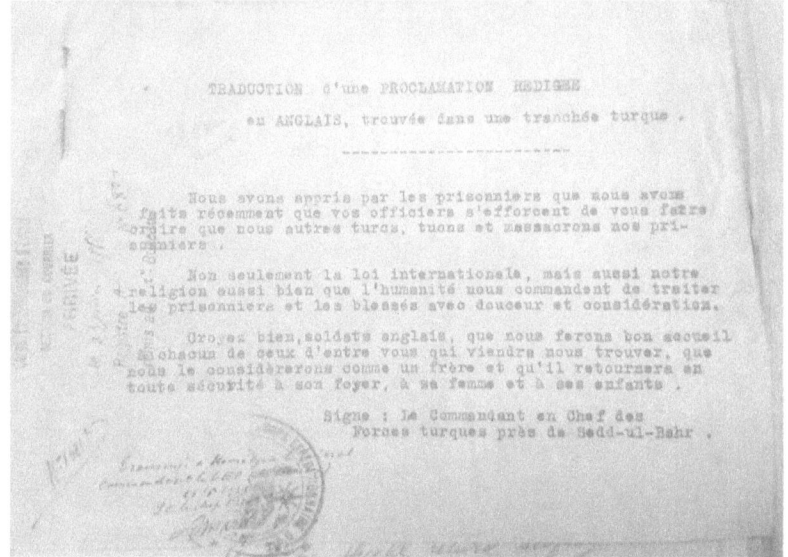

Document 12: The letter of the Turkish commander to occupying soldiers.[311]

Document 13: General Bailloud's order no. 905M.[312]

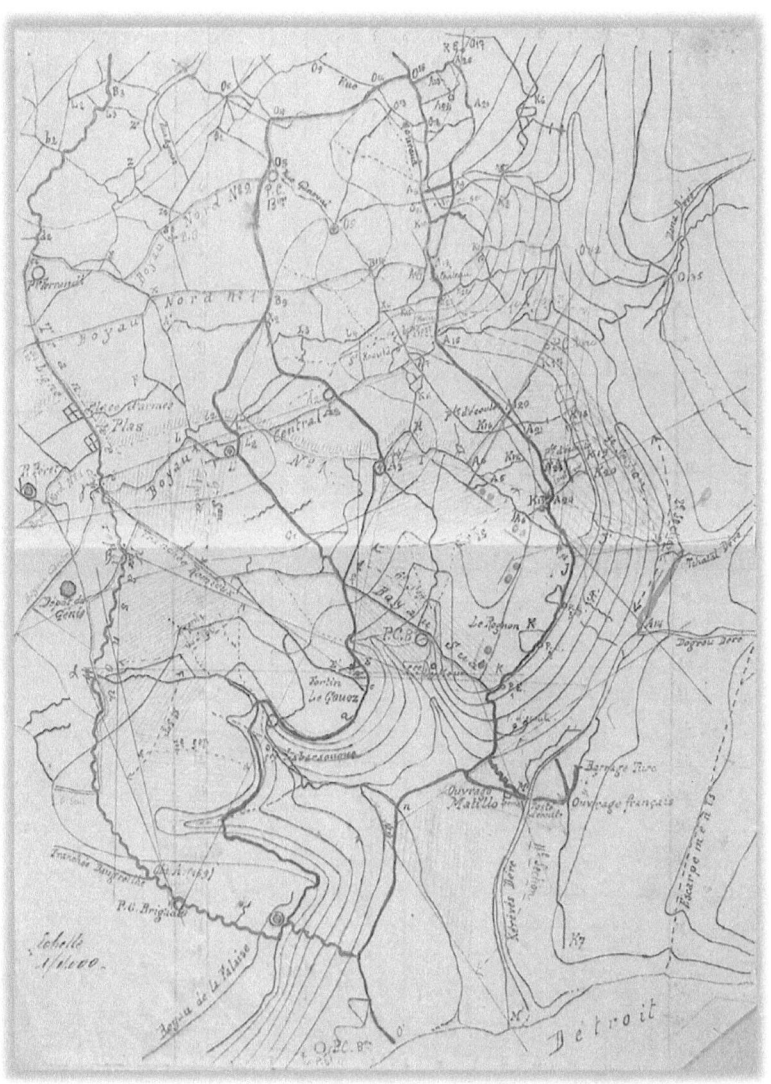

***Document 14:** French map showing the French trenches and communication lines at Yassıtepe and environs.*[313]

Biographies

Ahmet Nuri Diriker (Brigadier General, 1876-1951) He was born in Russe (now in Bulgaria). After attending middle school in Russe, he went to the Kuleli Military School. He graduated from the War Academy as lieutenant in 1896. He took part in the 1897 Greco-Turkish War and was the commander of the platoon which first entered Domokos. In the Balkans, he fought against the Albanian and Bulgarian revolts. In 1911, he was sent to Yemen as commander of the 4th Battalion of the 81st Regiment. He fought against the forces of Imam Yahya and Seyyid Idris in Yemen and Asir. He was promoted to the rank of major in recognition of his valor in the Djebelsob Battle. He took part in the Army of Action ('Hareket Ordusu'). In Gallipoli, he commanded the 42nd Regiment, which fought in Kerevizdere. He was sent to the Hejaz in 1916. Under his command, the 42nd Regiment broke through the siege of Medina and entered the city. In Medina, he fought under Lt. Gen. Fahreddin Pasha (General Türkkan), who later said of Ahmet Nuri: "He was a precious soldier in battlefields where Azrail (the Angel of Death) blew his trumpet". Under his command, the 42nd Regiment was twice awarded medals of honour. During the Armistice of Moudros, he was sent on a secret mission to İzmir and Aydın, from where he organized the shipment of military equipment to Anatolia. In 1921, he was ordered by the National Forces to come to Anatolia and join the War of Independence. He participated in the Battle of Sakarya as acting commander of the 23rd Division. He was then appointed as the commander of a brigade of the 8th Division. In 1922, he became the Chair of the

42nd Regiment

Second Military Court of the Western Front, and in 1923 he was appointed as the Chair of the Bolu Military Recruitment Department. After the proclamation of the Republic, he assumed various military positions in different parts of Turkey. He was promoted to Brigadier General in 1929 and took over the command of a brigade of the 7th Division. He retired in 1931 (Diriker, *Cephelerde Bir Ömür [A Life at the Fronts]*; Toker, *Çanakkale Muharebelerine Katılan Komutanların Biyografileri, [Biographies of Commanders Who Took Part in the Gallipoli War]* p.62-68).

Ahmet Süreyya (1872-unknown): He was born in Merzifon and graduated from the War Academy as lieutenant in 1896. He participated in the Balkan War and was taken prisoner in 1913. Upon his return, he was assigned to the 5th Corps. He was the commander of the 2nd Battalion of the 42nd Regiment at Gallipoli, and later became the commander of the 13th Regiment. He served as the commander of the Guard for the Hejaz Railway, and was wounded in Amman in 1918. He commanded the 33rd Regiment, and later joined the National Forces, which fought the Turkish War of Independence in 1920. He also took part in repressing the Zile Revolt (Toker & Aslan; *Birinci Dünya Savaşına Katılan Alay ve Daha Üst Kademedeki Komutanların Biyografileri [Biographies of regiment commanders and other higher rank commanders who took part in WW1]*, Vol. 2, p.214, 215; *42nd Regiment's War Diary*).

Ali Saib (Lt. Col, 1879-unknown): He graduated from the War Academy as lieutenant in 1890. He took part in the Tripoli War and commanded the 3rd Battalion of the 42nd Regiment in Gallipoli. He participated in the Hejaz War and was assigned as the commander of the 42nd Regiment at the end of 1916. He was taken POW after the fall of Medina in 1919 and sent to Egypt. After his return, he served as the head of the military recruitment offices in different parts of Anatolia (Toker & Aslan; ibid, p.42-43).

Fuad (Lt. Col., unknown-1915): He was born in Istanbul and graduated from the War Academy as lieutenant in 1892. He took part in the Tripoli War. He was the commander of the 41st Regiment in Gallipoli where he fell on 14 September 1915 (Toker, *Çanakkale Muharebelerine Katılan Komutanların Biyografileri [Biographies of Commanders Who Took Part in the Gallipoli War]*, p.176 - 177; *14th Division War Diary*).

Hasan Tahsin (Major; 1872-1915): He was born in Istanbul as the son of Halil Bey. He commanded the 55th Regiment during the Gallipoli War. He fell in Gallipoli on 21 August 1915 (Toker, ibid, p. 217; *14th Division's War Diary:* H12-001-013a).

Mehmet Tevfik (Colonel, 1876-unknown): He was born in Erzurum and graduated from the War Academy as lieutenant in 1895. He took part in the Balkan War and was the commander of the 1st Battalion of the 42nd Regiment in Gallipoli. He was wounded in the battlefield and was subsequently appointed as the commander of the 55th Regiment. Under his command, the regiment was sent to the Syrian Front. He was appointed as the Acting Commander of the 58th Division in 1918, and was taken prisoner in 1919. After his return, he participated in the Battle of Sakarya and the Great Offensive during the Turkish War of Independence (Toker, ibid, p.391, 392; Toker & Aslan, *Birinci Dünya Savaşına Katılan Alay ve Daha Üst Kademedeki Komutanların Biyografileri [Biographies of regiment commanders and other higher rank commanders who took part in WW1]*, Vol. 2, p.71,72; *42nd Regiment's War Diary*).

Osman Arif Ertürk (Colonel, 1878-unknown): He was born in Kızanlık and graduated from the War Academy as lieutenant in 1896. He took part in the 1897 Greco-Turkish War and the Balkan War. He was the commander of the 3rd Battalion of the 41st Regiment in Gallipoli. He also served as the commander of the 41st Regiment and the 142nd Regiment. He was taken as a POW by the British

42nd Regiment

while fighting at the Iraqi Front in 1917. After his return, he went to Anatolia to take part in the Turkish War of Independence. He commanded the 5th Regiment and later a brigade of the 17th Division. He worked as the head of military recruitment offices in various cities before retiring in 1930 (Toker & Aslan; ibid, Vol. 2, p.322, 323).

References

[1] Görgülü, *Çanakkale Muharebeleri'nin ve Komuta Kadrosunun Türk Kurtuluş Savaşı'na Etkileri*, Çanakkale Arastırmaları Türk Yıllığı 95'nci Yıl Özel Sayısı [*The Impact of the Gallipoli War and Its Command Staff on the Turkish War of Independence, Gallipoli Studies Turkish Annals, Special Issue For 95th Anniversary*], p.21.

[2] Koyuncu, Keskin, Sönmez, *Çanakkale Savaşları Bibliyografyası* [*Bibliography of the Gallipoli War*], p.XI.

[3] Erickson, *Gallipoli: The Ottoman Campaign*, p.11-13.

[4] *Birinci Dünya Savaşı'nda Çanakkale Cephesi* [*Gallipoli Front in WW1*], Vol.5, 2nd Book p. 4, 5.

[5] ibid. Vol.5, 3rd Book, p.122, 123.

[6] Artuç, *1915 Çanakkale Savaşı* [*1915 Gallipoli War*], p.247.

[7] *Birinci Dünya Savaşı'nda Çanakkale Cephesi* [*Gallipoli Front in WW1*], Vol.5, 3rd Book, p.127-139.

[8] ibid p.145.

[9] ibid p.139.

[10] ibid p.228, 242.

[11] ibid p.242.

[12] ibid p.245.

[13] ibid p.271.

[14] *Les Armées Françaises dans La Grande Guerre,* Tome VIII, 1er Volume Annexes 1er Volume, p. 455.

[15] ibid p. 462-463.

[16] *Birinci Dünya Savaşı'nda Çanakkale Cephesi* [*Gallipoli Front in WW1*], Vol. 5, 3rd Book, p.218.

[17] 14th Division's War Diary, H12-001-015.

[18] *Birinci Dünya Savaşı'nda Çanakkale Cephesi,* [*Gallipoli Front in WW1*], Vol. 5, 3rd Book, p.286.

[19] 14th Division's War Diary, H12-001-016.

[20] Diriker, *Cephelerde Bir Ömür Ahmet Nuri Diriker Paşa'nın Hatıratı* [*A Life at the Fronts: Memoirs of Ahmet Nuri Diriker Pasha*], p.53.

21 42nd Regiment's War Diary, H1-001-043.
22 ibid H1-001-043A.
23 Diriker, *Cephelerde Bir Ömür: Ahmet Nuri Diriker Paşa'nın Hatıratı [A Life at the Fronts: Memoirs of Ahmet Nuri Diriker Pasha]*, p.53.
24 *Birinci Dünya Savaşı'nda Çanakkale Cephesi [Gallipoli Front in WW1]*, Vol. 5, 3rd Book, p.262.
25 ibid p.265.
26 42nd Regiment's War Diary, H1-001-064a.
27 *Birinci Dünya Savaşı'nda Çanakkale Cephesi, [Gallipoli Front in WW1]*, Vol. 5, 3rd Book, p.262.
28 14th Division's War Diary, H7-001-20.
29 ibid H7-001-20.
30 42nd Regiment's War Diary, H1-001-66.
31 ibid H1-001-66a.
32 ibid H1-001-66a.
33 ibid H1-001-66, 66a.
34 ibid H1-001-66.
35 ibid H1-001-68a.
36 ibid H1-001-069.
37 ibid H1-001-069.
38 ibid H1-001-069a.
39 ibid H1-001-069a,70
40 ibid H1-001-070.
41 ibid H1-001-070a.
42 ibid H1-001-071.
43 ibid H1-001-70a.
44 55th Regiment's War Diary, H4-001-03.
45 ibid H6-001-02a.
46 ibid H7-001-02.
47 42nd Regiment's War Diary, H1-001-70a.
48 ibid H1-001-70a.
49 French 1st Divison's War Diary, 26N75-11.
50 French Expeditionary Corps of the Orient (CEO) War Diary, 26N75-5, p.207.
51 42nd Regiment's War Diary, H1-001-71.
52 ibid H1-001-71.
53 ibid H1-001-71a.

54 ibid H1-001-71a.
55 ibid H1-001-71.
56 ibid H1-001-71a.
57 ibid H1-001-71a.
58 ibid H1-001-72.
59 ibid H1-001-72.
60 ibid H1-001-72a.
61 ibid H1-001-73.
62 ibid H1-001-72a.
63 *Birinci Dünya Savaşı'nda Çanakkale Cephesi [Gallipoli Front in WW1]*, Vol. 5, 3rd Book, p.294-297
64 42nd Regiment's War Diary, H1-001-72a
65 ibid H1-001-73,73a.
66 14th Division's War Diary, H8- 001-36a.
67 42nd Regiment's War Diary, H1-001-074.
68 ibid H1-001-074.
69 Maps (from the French Military Archive), 20N28.
70 42nd Regiment's War Diary, H1-001-088.
71 ibid H1-001-074.
72 ibid H1-001-074a.
73 ibid H1-001-074a.
74 ibid H1-001-074a.
75 ibid H1-001-075, 088.
76 ibid H1-001-088.
77 ibid H1-001-75.
78 55th Regiment's War Diary, H6-001-03
79 42nd Regiment's War Diary, H1-001-075a
80 ibid H1-001-075a.
81 14th Division's War Diary, H11-001-01
82 ibid H11-001-01a, 02.
83 ibid H11-001-02.
84 42nd Regiment's War Diary, H1-001-076.
85 ibid H1-001-076.
86 ibid H1-001-076.
87 14th Division's War Diary, H11-001-03.
88 42nd Regiment's War Diary, H1-001-078.
89 ibid H1-001-076A.

42nd Regiment

[90] 14th Division's War Diary, H11-001-02.
[91] 42nd Regiment's War Diary, H1-088a.
[92] ibid H1-001-078a.
[93] 14th Division's War Diary, H11-001-02a.
[94] 42nd Regiment's War Diary, H1-001-078a, 79.
[95] ibid H1-001-078a.
[96] 41st Regiment's War Diary, 001-03a.
[97] 42nd Regiment's War Diary, H1-001-79.
[98] ibid H1-001-079a.
[99] ibid H1-001-078a.
[100] ibid H1-001-080.
[101] ibid H1-001-080.
[102] ibid H1-001-80a.
[103] ibid H1-001-080a.
[104] ibid H1-001-081.
[105] Ibid H1-001-081.
[106] Ibid H1-001-081a.
[107] Harp Mecmuası *[War Journal]*, no. 4.
[108] 42nd Regiment's War Diary H1-001-081a.
[109] ibid H1-001-082a.
[110] ibid H1-001-082a.
[111] 14th Division's War Diary, H9-001-23.
[112] 42nd Regiment's War Diary, H1-001-085.
[113] ibid H1-001-086a.
[114] Harp Mecmuası *[War Journal]*, no. 17.
[115] 42nd Regiment's War Diary, H1-001-86.
[116] ibid H1-001-86a.
[117] ibid H1-001-87.
[118] ibid H1-001-084a.
[119] ibid H1-001-090.
[120] ibid H1-001-087a.
[121] French CEO, Report no 920M, dated 8 August 1915.
[122] French 1st Divison's War Diary, 26N75-11.
[123] Vassal, *Uncensored Letters from the Dardenelles*, p.173,174.
[124] ibid p.174.
[125] Roux, *L'Expedition des Dardanelles*, p.78.

[126] 42nd Regiment's War Diary, H1-001-093.
[127] ibid H1-001-90a.
[128] Ibid H1-001-90a.
[129] ibid H1-001-091a.
[130] Harp Mecmuası [War Journal], no. 5.
[131] 42nd Regiment's War Diary, H1-001-091a.
[132] ibid H1-001-091a.
[133] ibid H1-001-092.
[134] ibid H1-001-092a.
[135] French 1st Divison's War Diary, 26N75-11.
[136] Vassal, Uncensored Letters from the Dardenelles, p.157-159.
[137] French 1st Divison's War Diary, 26N75-11.
[138] French CEO's War Diary, 26N75-5, p. 202.
[139] ibid 26N75-4, p.161.
[140] French 1st Divison's War Diary, 26N75-11.
[141] ibid 26N75-11.
[142] French CEO Report no 924M, dated 9.8.1915, 16N1205.
[143] 42nd Regiment's War Diary, H1-001-93a.
[144] ibid H1-001-094.
[145] French CEO Report dated 10.8.1915, no 939M, 20N28.
[146] French 1st Division's War Diary, 26N75-11.
[147] French CEO's War Diary, 26N75-5, p.222.
[148] ibid 26N75-5, p.222.
[149] 42nd Regiment's War Diary, H1-001-95.
[150] 55th Regiment's War Diary, 1-001-21.
[151] 42nd Regiment's War Diary, H1-001-95a.
[152] ibid H1-001-95a.
[153] ibid H1-001-096.
[154] ibid H1-001-096.
[155] ibid H1-001-096a.
[156] 14th Division's War Diary, H11-001-014.
[157] ibid H11-001-014.
[158] Birinci Dünya Savaşı'nda Çanakkale Cephesi [Gallipoli Front in WW1], Vol. 5, 3rd Book, p.306.
[159] 42nd Regiment's War Diary, H1-001-098.
[160] ibid H1-001-99a.

42nd Regiment

[161] 14th Division's War Diary, H12-001-014.
[162] 42nd Regiment's War Diary, H1-001-99a and 100.
[163] ibid H1-001-100.
[164] 42nd Regiment's War Diary H1-001-100.
[165] French 1st Division's War Diary, 26N75-11.
[166] 42nd Regiment's War Diary, H1-001-100.
[167] 14th Division's War Diary, H12-001-014.
[168] 42nd Regiment's War Diary, H1-001-100; 14th Division War Diary, H12-001-014.
[169] 42nd Regiment's War Diary, H1-001-100a.
[170] ibid H1-001-101.
[171] 14th Division's War Diary, H12-001-014a.
[172] ibid H12-001-014a.
[173] ibid H12-001-014a
[174] ibid H12-001-08.
[175] ibid H12-001-013a.
[176] ibid H12-001-013a.
[177] ibid H12-001-018a.
[178] 42nd Regiment's War Diary, H1-001-101a.
[179] ibid H1-001-101a.
[180] 14th Division's War Diary, H12-001-015.
[181] ibid H12-001-015.
[182] ibid H12-001-015a.
[183] ibid H12-001-015a.
[184] ibid H12-001-016.
[185] ibid H12-001-016.
[186] ibid H12-001-016.
[187] ibid H12-001-017, 017a.
[188] 42nd Regiment's War Diary, H1-001-103.
[189] ibid H1-001-103; 14th Division's War Diary, H13-001-002a.
[190] 14th Division's War Diary, H12-001-19.
[191] French CEO's War Diary, 26N75-5, p.236.
[192] 42nd Regiment's War Diary, H1-001-103.
[193] 14th Division's War Diary, H13-001-002a.
[194] 42nd Regiment's War Diary, H1-001-103.
[195] ibid H1-001-103.

[196] French CEO's War Diary, 26N75-5, p. 237.
[197] ibid 26N75-5, p.237.
[198] 42nd Regiment's War Diary, H1-001-103a.
[199] French CEO's War Diary, 26N75-5, p. 237.
[200] 42nd Regiment's War Diary, H1-001-104.
[201] 14th Division's War Diary, H13-001-006a.
[202] ibid H13-001-006a.
[203] ibid H13-001-006a.
[204] ibid H13-001-006a, 007.
[205] ibid H13-001-007.
[206] ibid H13-001-006.
[207] 42nd Regiment's War Diary, H1-001-104.
[208] French 1st Division's War Diary, 26N75-11.
[209] 42nd Regiment's War Diary, H1-001-104a.
[210] ibid H1-001-104a.
[211] ibid H1-001- 104a, 106.
[212] ibid H1-001-106.
[213] ibid H1-001-106.
[214] ibid H1-001-106a.
[215] ibid H1-001-106a.
[216] ibid H1-001-107.
[217] French CEO's War Diary, 26N75-5, p.241.
[218] Vassal, *Uncensored Letters from the Dardenelles*, p.181.
[219] French CEO's War Diary, 26N75-5, p.242.
[220] Oglander, *Military Operations - Gallipoli,* Vol.2, p.141.
[221] French CEO Operation Report no 1221M, dated 1 Oct. 1915, 20N28.
[222] 42nd Regiment's War Diary, H1-001-107a,108.
[223] Order no1064M, dated 31 Aug. 1915, 20N28.
[224] 42nd Regiment's War Diary, H1-001-109.
[225] 14th Division's War Diary, H13-001-24.
[226] ibid H13-001-21a.
[227] 42nd Regiment's War Diary, H1-001-99.
[228] 55th Regiment's War Diary, H6-001-03.
[229] Görgülü, *Çanakkale Muharebeleri'nin ve Komuta Kadrosunun Türk Kurtuluş Savaşı'na Etkileri [The Impact of the Gallipoli War and Its*

Command Staff on the Turkish War of Independence, Gallipoli Studies Turkish Annals, Special Issue For 95th Anniversary], p.18.
[230] Vassal, *Uncensored Letters from the Dardenelles*, p.185.
[231] Görgülü, *Çanakkale Muharebeleri'nin ve Komuta Kadrosunun Türk Kurtuluş Savaşı'na Etkileri [The Impact of the Gallipoli War and Its Command Staff on Turkish War of Liberation, Gallipoli Studies Turkish Annals Special Issue For 95th Anniversary]*, p.16.
[232] 42nd Regiment's War Diary, H1-001-086.
[233] Diriker, *Cephelerde Bir Ömür Ahmet Nuri Diriker Paşa'nın Hatıratı [A Life at the Fronts: Memoirs of Ahmet Nuri Diriker Pasha]*, p.57.
[234] 14th Division's War Diary, H15-001-012a.
[235] ibid H15-001-012a.
[236] ibid H15-001-012a.
[237] Harp Mecmuası *[War Journal]*, sayı 19.
[238] 14th Division's War Diary, H15-001-012a.
[239] ibid H15-001-012a.
[240] 42nd Regiment's War Diary, H1-001-112a.
[241] ibid H1-001-115.
[242] ibid H1-001-115.
[243] ibid H1-001-115a.
[244] 14th Division's War Diary, H15-001-18.
[245] ibid H15-001-18.
[246] 42nd Regiment's War Diary, H1-001-117.
[247] ibid H1-001- 118, 119.
[248] Harp Mecmuası *[War Journal]*, no. 4.
[249] 42nd Regiment's War Diary, H1-001-119.
[250] French CEO's Operation Report no 1221M, 20N28.
[251] French CEO's War Diary, 26N75-6 p.259.
[252] French CEO's Operation Report no 1141M, dated 16 Sep. 1915, 20N28.
[253] 42nd Regiment's War Diary, H1-001-117a.
[254] French CEO's War Diary, 26N75-6, p.260.
[255] ibid p.266.
[256] French CEO's Operation Report no 1221M, dated 1 Oct. 1915, 20N28.
[257] *Birinci Dünya Savaşı'nda Çanakkale Cephesi [Gallipoli Front in WW1]*, p.446-447.
[258] *Les Armées Françaises Dans La Grande Guerre*, Tome VIII, 1er Volume, Annex, p.596.

[259] *Les Armées Françaises Dans La Grande Guerre,* Tome VIII, 1er Volume, p. 115.
[260] *Les Armées Françaises Dans La Grande Guerre,* Tome VIII, 1er Volume, Annex, p.604.
[261] 42nd Regiment's War Diary, H1-001-120a.
[262] ibid H1-001-120a.
[263] ibid H1-001-120a.
[264] French CEO's War Diary, 26N75-6, p.285.
[265] 42nd Regiment's War Diary, H1-001-120a.
[266] French CEO's War Diary, 26N75-6, p.288.
[267] 42nd Regiment's War Diary, H1-001-121.
[268] ibid H1-001-121.
[269] ibid H1-001-121.
[270] ibid H1-001-121a.
[271] ibid H1-001-121a.
[272] French CEO's War Diary, 26N75-6, p.291.
[273] ibid 26N75-6 p.293.
[274] ibid 26N75-6 p.294.
[275] ibid 26N75-6 p.296
[276] 42nd Regiment's War Diary, H1-001-125.
[277] ibid H1-001-127.
[278] ibid H1-001-127a.
[279] ibid H1-001-127a.
[280] ibid H1-001-126.
[281] ibid H1-001-128.
[282] ibid H1-001-128.
[283] French CEO's War Diary, 26N75-7, p.307.
[284] ibid 26N75-7 p.307.
[285] ibid 26N75-7 p.310.
[286] ibid 26N75-7 p.312.
[287] ibid 26N75-7 p. 319.
[288] 14th Division's War Diary, H15-001-17.
[289] 42nd Regiment's War Diary, H1-001-133.
[290] ibid H1-001-133.
[291] ibid H1-001-135a.
[292] Vassal, *Uncensored Letters from the Dardenelles,* p.179.

[293] *Birinci Dünya Savaşı'nda Çanakkale Cephesi [Gallipoli Front in WW1]*, Vol.5, Book 3, p.439.
[294] French Expeditionary Corps of the Dardanelles (CED) Operation Report no.1470, 20N28.
[295] Diriker, *Cephelerde Bir Ömür: Ahmet Nuri Diriker Paşa'nın Hatıratı, [A Life at the Fronts: Memoirs of Ahmet Nuri Diriker Pasha]* p.66.
[296] ibid p.57.
[297] Ibid p.67.
[298] ibid p.248-251.
[299] Pamukoğlu, *Unutulanlar Dışında Yeni Bir Şey Yok, [Nothing New Except What Is Forgotten]* p.20-22.
[300] CEO & CED, 20N52.
[301] 42nd Regiment's War Diary, H1-001-077.
[302] ibid H1-001-079A.
[303] Maps (from the French Military Archives), 20N543.
[304] French 2nd Brigade's map, 20N28.
[305] French 56th Colonial Regiment's trench report, 20N28.
[306] French 56th Colonial Regiment's trench report, 25N543.
[307] 42nd Regiment's War Diary, H1-001-108.
[308] ibid, H1-001-116.
[309] French 1st Brigade, 20N52.
[310] French CEO Operation Report no. 979, dated 16.8.1915, 20N28.
[311] Correspondance (French Archives), 25N543.
[312] French CEO's Operation Instructions, 20N23.
[313] Maps (French Archives), 25N543.

Bibliography

Archives du Service Historique de l'Armee de Terre, Chateau de Vincennes, *(all French war diaries, reports, maps, diagrams, correspondence related to the Gallipoli Front).*

Artuç, İ. 2004. *1915 Çanakkale Savaşı [1915 Gallipoli War]*, Kastaş Yayınevi.

Birinci Dünya Harbi'nde Türk Harbi [The Turkish War in WW1], Vol.5, Book 3, 1980, Genkur. Basımevi.

Birinci Dünya Savaşı'nda Çanakkale Cephesi, [Gallipoli Front in WW1] Vol. 5, Book 2, 2012, Genkur ATASE Daire Başkanlığı Yayınları.

Birinci Dünya Savaşı'nda Çanakkale Cephesi, [Gallipoli Front in WW1] Vol. 5, Book 3, 2012, Genkur ATASE Daire Başkanlığı Yayınları.

Bull, S. 2014. *Trench: A History of Trench Warfare on the Western Front*, ebook

Diriker, A. *2009. Cephelerde bir Ömür: Ahmet Nuri Diriker Paşa'nın Hatıratı [A Life at The Fronts: Memoirs of Ahmet Nuri Diriker Pasha]*, Scala Yayıncılık.

Erickson E.J. 2010, *Gallipoli: The Ottoman Campaign,* Pen & Sword Military.

Turkish General Staff, Military History and Strategic Studies (ATASE) Archive, WW1 Collection, (War diaries, diagrams, correspondence, etc.).

Görgülü, İ. 2010. *Çanakkale Muharebeleri'nin ve Komuta Kadrosunun Türk Kurtuluş Savaşı'na Etkileri [The Impact of the Gallipoli War and Its Command Staff on the Turkish War of Independence, Gallipoli Studies Turkish Annals, Special Issue for the 95th Anniversary]* Vol. 8-9, Çanakkale Onsekiz Mart University.

Harp Mecmuası [War Journal], Ministry of Defence.

Kıcıman, N.K. 1994. *Medine Müdafaası [Medina Defence]*, Sebil Yayınevi.

Koyuncu, A. Keskin Ö. Sönmez, C. 2010. *Çanakkale Savaşları Bibliyografyası [Bibliography of the Gallipoli Wars]*, Atatürk Arastırma Merkezi.

Le portail de la généalogie en France, http://memorial-genweb.org/~b1914-1918/resultpatro.php

Les Armées Françaises Dans La Grande Guerre, Tome VIII 1er Volume, Annexes 1er Volume.

Mehmet Şevki Paşa. 2009. *Çanakkale Tahkimat Haritası [Fortification Map of the Dardanelles]*, Genkur ATASE Daire Başkanlığı.

Letter number *45012883-7940-3379 dated 02.8.2015* of the Ministery of Defence, Directorate of Archives.

Oglander, A. 1962. *Çanakkale Gelibolu Askeri Harekâtı [Military Operations - Gallipoli]*, Vol. 2, Askeri Matbaa.

Pamukoğlu, O. 2004. *Unutulanlar Dışında Yeni Bir Şey Yok [Nothing New Except What Is Forgotten]*, İnkılap Yayınevi.

Roux, C. 1920. *L'Expedition des Dardanelles*, Armand Colin.

Sayılır, B. 2008. *Tarihe Sığmayanlar, Çanakkale Savaşı'nın Şehit Subayları [Exceeding History, The Fallen Officers of the Gallipoli War]*, Phoenix Kitapevi.

Sanders, L. von. 2007. *Türkiye'de Beş Sene [Five Years in Turkey]*, Yeditepe Yayınevi.

Toker, H. Aslan, N. 2009. *Birinci Dünya Savaşına Katılan Alay ve Daha Üst Kademedeki Komutanların Biyografileri [Biographies of regiment commanders and other higher rank commanders who took part in WW1]*, Genkur. ATASE Başkanlığı Yayınları.

Toker, H. 2014. *Çanakkale Muharebelerine Katılan Komutanların Biyografileri [Biographies of the Commanders who took part in the Gallipoli War]*, Genkur ATASE Daire Başkanlığı Yayınları.

Vassal, J.M.J. 1916. *Uncensored Letters from the Dardanelles*, William Heinneman.

Index

1

1st African Regiment (French), 34, 35, 36, 82, 92, 97

2nd African Regiment (French), 34, 35

1st Division (French), 26, 34, 35, 36, 59, 69, 71, 93, 112, 145

10th Division (Turkish), 24, 39, 40, 109

13th Division (Turkish), 24, 40, 73

14th Division (Turkish), 25, 26, 27, 28, 29, 33, 34, 36, 40, 52, 56, 57, 58, 73, 74, 84, 86, 87, 88, 92, 97, 98, 99, 104, 107, 111, 112, 116, 118, 122, 125, 128, 129, 138, 153

175th Regiment (French), 34, 35, 36, 59, 82, 97, 114

176th Regiment (French), 35, 35, 36, 114

2

2nd Division (French), 22, 25, 26, 34, 35, 36, 60, 71, 115

2nd Division (Turkish), 20, 21

4

4th Division (Turkish), 22, 25

4th Colonial Regiment (later 54th Colonial Reg.- French), 35, 61, 71, 78

41st Regiment (Turkish), 27, 29, 32, 33, 38, 40, 43, 46, 48, 53, 56, 58, 59, 64, 68, 78, 86, 89, 103, 109, 110, 111, 116, 118, 153, 154

5

5th Army (Turkish), 24, 28

5th Corp (Turkish), 24, 28, 29, 88, 90, 104, 152

54th Colonial Reg.(frm 4th Colonial Reg.- French), 71, 81, 97,

55th Regiment (Turkish), 29, 31, 33, 34, 36, 40, 42, 44, 45, 51, 56, 57, 63, 71, 72, 74, 77, 87, 89, 93, 105, 108,137, 143,153

56th Colonial Reg. (frm 6th Colonial Rgt.- French), 71, 81, 97, 141, 142

6

6th Colonial Regiment (later 56th Colonial Reg.- French), 35, 61, 71

A

Ahmet Nuri (Diriker), 14, 27, 29, 30, 31, 33, 38, 40, 42, 43, 44, 46, 47, 48, 49, 52, 53, 54, 58, 65, 66, 67, 72, 74, 81, 95, 96, 104, 107, 110, 111, 116, 125, 128, 129, 138, 151, 165

Ahmet Süreyya (2nd Bn Cmd), 32, 37, 38, 39, 46, 47, 50, 52, 53, 55, 56, 152

B

Bailloud, 22, 34, 35, 59, 69, 101, 103, 115, 148

blockhouse, 75, 77, 78, 79, 80, 81, 91, 94, 95, 97, 98, 99, 100, 103, 104, 109, 110, 115, 117, 118, 119, 122, 123, 139

Brulard, 69, 115

C

caltrop, 83, 84

camouflet, 76, 113

Cesaret Cliff, 34

Cesetlertepe, 34, 36, 37, 118, 120

Corps Expéditionnaire des Dardanelles (C.E.D.), 115

Corps Expéditionnaire d'Orient (C.E.O.), 20, (see also Expeditionary Corps of the Orient)

D

Dardanelles, 11, 16, 18, 19, 22, 24, 34, 35, 36, 37, 115, 131

E

Esat Pasha (Bülkat), 28, 89

Expeditionary Corps of the Orient (C.E.O.), 20, 24, 25, 34, 78, 105, 115

F

Fahreddin Pasha (Türkkan), 132, 151

Fevzi Pasha (Çakmak), 29, 96, 114

Fuad (41st Rgt Cmdr), 14, 110, 111, 112, 131, 153

Fuadbey Deresi (River), 110 (see also İsimsizdere)

G

Gazilertepe (Hill), 56, 86

Gouraud, 20, 22, 34, 101

H

Hamilton, 20, 23, 24, 38, 39, 101

Hasan Tahsin (55th Rgt Cmdr), 51, 56, 72, 74, 86, 153

Hejaz Expeditionary Force, 132

Hüseyin Avni, 133

I

İldere, 34, 35, 36, 88

İsimsizdere, 34, 36, 37, 40, 59, 118 (see also Fuadbey Deresi)

Kanlıdere, 20, 21, 22, 23, 25, 26, 35, 39,

K

Kansızdere, 33, 34, 36, 37, 39, 49, 58, 68, 82, 87, 97, 98, 112, 114, 116, 118, 123 (see also Ravin de la Mort)

Kâzım (Karabekir), 27, 29, 30, 40, 49, 57, 65, 67, 70, 74, 86, 88, 92, 96, 97, 99, 108, 109, 111, 114, 116, 122, 129

Kemalbey Tepesi (Hill), 20, 21, 22

Kerevizdere, 12, 13, 19, 20, 21, 22, 25, 31, 33, 34, 35, 36, 39, 40, 41, 42, 43, 44, 52, 56, 58, 67, 68, 69, 72, 73, 74, 75, 78, 80, 81, 82, 83, 84, 85, 87, 88, 90, 91, 93, 94, 96, 97, 98, 104, 109, 110, 119, 123, 129, 130, 137, 140, 143

Kudsi (55th Rgt 1st Bn Cmdr), 56

Kudsibey Hill (Tepesi), 56, 71, 108, 122

L

Lahnadere, 36, 37, 104

Liman von Sanders, 28, 114, 167

M

Masnou, 69, 104, 118

Matillo, 78, 79, 80, 94, 100, 104, 118, 119

Mediterranean Expeditionary Force, 19, 20, 24

Mehmet Ali (1st Bn Cmdr), 46, 54

Millerand, 101

Mustafa Kemal (Atatürk), 11, 13, 19, 106

N

Nuri Bey Fountain, 128, 130

O

Osman (Ertürk), 45, 46, 48, 51, 52, 58, 64, 65, 70, 72, 78, 82, 83, 84, 86, 87, 111, 153

R

Ravin de la Mort, 33, (see also Kansızdere)

Rıza Hayreddin (40th MG Coy Cmdr), 33, 39, 53, 54, 65

Rognon, 22 [see also Yassıtepe]

Roux, 63, 166

S

Saib (3rd Bn Cmdr), 66, 152

sap, 70, 103, 117, 118, 119

Schwartz, 35, 60, 69

Seddulbahir, 12, 17, 18, 19, 20, 21, 23, 24, 25, 38, 63, 70, 75, 114, 115, 123, 127

Sodenstern (von), 122, 128, 129

Soğanlıdere, 28, 31, 87, 99, 110, 128, 129

Suvla, 23, 62, 101, 127

Şüheda Tepe, 34, 36, 37, 118, 124

T

Tevfik (55th Rgt Cmdr), 32, 46, 87, 116, 153

V

Vassal, 22, 61, 69, 100, 105, 126

Vehip Pasha (Kaçi), 28, 29, 90, 114

Y

Yassı Tepe, 22, 35, 37, 38, 39, 40, 41, 43, 52, 53, 55, 56, 57, 58, 59, 60, 64, 65, 66, 71, 72, 77, 83, 84, 87, 91, 92, 93, 95, 105, 112, 117, 123, 149, (see also Rognon)

Z

Zığındere, 12, 19, 21, 39

www.ingramcontent.com/pod-product-compliance
Lightning Source LLC
Chambersburg PA
CBHW020908080526
44589CB00011B/489